UNDERSTANDING FAITH

AKIN AKINYEMI

SYNCTERFACE™
Syncterface Media
London
www.syncterfacemedia.com

Unless otherwise indicated, all Scripture quotations in this book are taken from the King James Version of the Holy Bible. Scriptures marked NKJV are taken from the New King James Version®. Copyright © 1982 by Thomas Nelson. Scriptures marked GWT are taken from God's Word Translation Copyright © 1995 by God's Word to the Nations. Used by permission of Baker Publishing Group. Scriptures marked AMP are from The Amplified Bible Copyright © 1954, 1958, 1962, 1964, 1965, 1987 by The Lockman Foundation
(Capitalised text and italics may be used for emphasis)
Used by permission.

No part of this book may be reproduced or transmitted in any form or by any means, graphic, electronic, or mechanical, including photocopying, recording, taping or by any information storage or retrieval system, without the permission of the author.

UNDERSTANDING FAITH

ISBN: 978-0-9933860-1-5
Copyright © October 2015
Akin Akinyemi
All Rights Reserved

Published in the United Kingdom by

SYNCTERFACE™

Syncterface Media
London
www.syncterfacemedia.com
info@syncterfacemedia.com

Cover Design: Syncterface Media, London

This book is printed on acid-free paper

CONTENTS

ACKNOWLEDGEMENTS

To Pastor Uvie Brigue

&

Members of Covenant Christian Centre, UK.

Thank you for supporting the mandate.

May God reward your labour of love and multiply you richly.

PULPIT TO BOOKSTORE

PULPIT TO BOOKSTORE BOOKS ARE BOOKS THAT HAVE BEEN TRANSCRIBED, LARGELY, FROM MESSAGES THAT WERE PREACHED OR TAUGHT BY THE AUTHOR AND ADAPTED FOR THE READING AUDIENCE.

SYNCTERFACE MEDIA, THEREFORE, WORKS WITH AUTHORS TO PRESERVE THE CONTEXT OF WHAT WAS DELIVERED DURING THE MESSAGE. IN MOST CASES, CHAPTERS CAN BE READ INDEPENDENT OF EACH OTHER.

BELIEVER'S FAITH CAMPAIGN: THE MANDATE

The Believer's Faith Campaign is a program that was born by the Spirit of God to achieve a mission to, *"restore faith to the land,"* given to its convener, Akin Akinyemi. The Lord spoke and said, *"...The cry of the people of the Land had come up to Me, many will not get healed if My other servants do not come. I want to raise a people in the land, who will carry My power in demonstrations of the Spirit, gifts of the Holy Spirit in healings and miracles through a balanced teaching of the Word of God...."*

Akin, who was commissioned into ministry by Pastor E. A. Adeboye, the General Overseer of the Redeemed Christian Church of God, noted that there is no place in the UK where the testimony of Jesus in *Matthew 11: 4-5* is fulfilled on a regular basis.

> *¹ And it came to pass, when Jesus had made an end of commanding his twelve disciples, he departed thence to teach and to preach in their cities.*
>
> *² Now when John had heard in the prison the works of Christ, he sent two of his disciples,*
>
> *³ And said unto him, Art thou he that should come, or do we look for another?*
>
> *⁴ **Jesus answered and said unto them, Go and shew John again those things which ye do hear and see:***
>
> *⁵ **The blind receive their sight, and the lame walk, the lepers are cleansed, and the deaf hear, the dead are raised up, and the poor have the gospel preached to them.***

Matthew 11: 1-5

The cry of People in the land has come up to God and He is saying that He is Jesus, the same yesterday, today and forever. He is still *"taking infirmities and bearing sicknesses"* that He may prove it is the good and acceptable will of God for the people to be made whole. The provision God made has not expired. The deal is still on and will remain on till Jesus returns and the last enemy, death, is destroyed.

The Believer's Faith Campaign seeks to address this imbalance. The UK has a very rich history of revivals and moves of the Holy Spirit but this is something the current generation of Christians seem not to be aware of. Operations of the Holy Spirit that are grounded and rooted in the Scriptures. Not emotional sensations but clear demonstrations of the Spirit and of power. Not enticing words of man's wisdom but demonstrations of the Spirit and power, all done while showing the character of Christ.

The Campaign seeks to:

1. *Create an avenue for people in the UK to be reminded of the rich heritage of revivals and that God has not turned his back on this nation*

2. *Demonstrate that the gospel of Jesus is not confined to financial prosperity and spiritual healing. It also addresses physical healing of all manner of sickness and disease through the balanced teaching of the Word of God*

3. *Create a platform for unleashing a remnant of ministers that the world has not heard of but God recognises*

4. *Stimulate faith in people through the operation of the gifts of the Holy Spirit as we recognise the Holy Spirit as the governing force of Heaven in operation in the Christian today*

5. *Create an atmosphere of worship that attracts the glory of God*

God gave specific instructions concerning the Campaign. It was to be interdenominational focussing on the teaching of the Word of God, the preaching of the Gospel, special sessions for praying for the sick and the demonstrations of the Holy Spirit. The primary audience is Believers but anyone with sickness or disease could attend and be healed of their sicknesses and diseases.

Many Christians in the land, have only been exposed to the gospel that predominantly addressees one of the areas in the response

Jesus gave. "*The gospel being preached to the poor.*" What about the blind who want sight and the lame who want to walk? What about the deaf who would love to hear? What about the people who want their dead raised up? At best, the Church of today will address these areas using them as spiritual metaphors. In *Matthew 9:35*, Jesus went about all the cities and villages, teaching in their synagogues, preaching the gospel of the kingdom and healing every sickness and every disease among the people. The message of the gospel is incomplete if we do not have the three components of *preaching*, *teaching* and *healing*, with the healing part not only confined to the far and deep healing of the broken heart but reaching as near as the healing of a broken body.

The Church, in many parts, is no longer considered as a place you can take the physically sick and trust God for their healing. Even when physical sickness is addressed, we address the lack of healing as a deficiency in the people, that is, their lack of faith and even more concerning in some circles, it is seen as the unwillingness of God to want to address the situation.

Mark 9:14-29 describes the story of a man with a son who had a dumb spirit that the disciples of Jesus could not cast out. In this case, it was not the faith of the man or the faith of his son that caused the disciples not to be able to cast out the devil. I believe that by coming to the disciples and, by proxy, Jesus, they had already exercised their faith. All that was left at this point was the faith, fasting and prayers of the disciples.

Healing of the physical body goes beyond just the faith of the sick one. It extends to the faith of the whole person who is in a position to administer healing as commanded by Jesus. Perhaps, the sick remains sick not because of their lack of faith but as a result of the lack of faith of the whole person. *James 5:14-15* declares, "*Is any sick among you? Let him call for the elders....and the prayer of faith shall save the sick, and the Lord shall raise him up;...*" The sick had already exercised faith by calling for the elders. In *Matthew 8:16-17*, the Bible says, "*.....they brought unto him many that were possessed with devils: and he cast out the spirits with his word, and healed all that were sick: that it might be fulfilled.......Himself took our infirmities, and bare our sicknesses.*" This should be the testimony of the Church today.

The Church should be perceived as a place where people can bring their sick ones so the prayer of faith can be offered, those possessed with devils come with an expectation that the devils will be cast out and those with diseases expect to be cured of the diseases. All these, while presenting the balanced gospel of the kingdom which is able to save and deliver anyone who calls to God for salvation.

Chapter 1

THINGS HOPED FOR

¹ Therefore leaving the principles of the doctrine of Christ, let us go on unto perfection; not laying again the foundation of repentance from dead works, and of faith toward God,
² Of the doctrine of baptisms, and of laying on of hands, and of resurrection of the dead, and of eternal judgment.
³ And this will we do, if God permit.

Hebrews 6:1-3 (KJV)

The writer of the book of Hebrews, in chapter 6, points us to some principles that Christians should embrace and be grounded in as they move towards the deeper things of God. While these principles are important, the writer, by using the word "leaving," suggests these principles are rather foundational ones that Christians need to build on. Christians should be on a journey to maturity. The rendition of these verses in the Amplified Bible makes the text even more enlightening.

¹ Therefore let us go on and get past the elementary stage in the teachings and doctrine of Christ (the Messiah), advancing steadily toward the completeness and perfection that belong to spiritual maturity. Let us not again be laying the foundation of repentance and abandonment of dead works (dead formalism) and of the faith [by which you turned] to God,
² With teachings about purifying, the laying on of hands, the resurrection from the dead, and eternal judgment and punishment. [These are all matters of which you should have been fully aware long, long ago.]
³ If indeed God permits, we will [now] proceed [to advanced teaching].

Hebrews 6:1-3 (AMP)

Relax! We are not going into any advanced teaching this morning. We need to revisit the foundations. Looking around us today, it is obvious that many Christians are frustrated; the results they achieve do not really depict the God they represent and people are turning to worldly principles for the attainment of the things of God.

This morning, I want to deal with the first two principles repentance from dead works and of faith toward God. However, I want to start with *"Faith towards God"* and within this, deal with *"repentance from dead works."*

Let us look at *Hebrews 11:1-3*. This whole chapter probably has the most classic definition of faith Christians have, as well as examples of people who achieved great things through the operation of faith in their own personal lives.

> [1]*Now faith is the substance of things hoped for, the evidence of things not seen.*
> [2] *For by it the elders obtained a good report.*
> [3] *Through faith we understand that the worlds were framed by the word of God, so that things which are seen were not made of things which do appear.*
>
> *Hebrews 11:1-3*

From *verse 1* we see two definitions of faith that we will want to look at in a bit more detail.

1. Faith is the substance of things hoped for

2. Faith is the evidence of things not seen

Faith is the substance of things hoped for

A lot of times, I like to unpack the scriptures and repack them so I can gain a full understanding of the hidden messages in them. So looking at the first statement, we see 3 things worth looking at individually.

1. Faith is

2. The substance of

3. Things hoped for

From the literal Greek, the word *"faith"* really means *"Persuasion of religious truth or the truthfulness of God"* while *"substance"* denotes *"having something set under"* or *"having support to stand or lean on."* This means when the writer of Hebrews tells us that "faith is the substance of things hoped for", the writer is making us understand that;

Faith is having a persuasion of a religious truth (or revelation as we call it these days) concerning what we are hoping for while having something as a support to lean on.

If this be the case, we need to carefully determine "what we hope for" and what we are leaning on for support because we could either hope for the wrong things or lean on something that is not really steady for support. This could mean we attract the wrong things into our lives or the right things we build crumble due to inadequate support.

It is crucial for us to remember that the principle being talked about in *Hebrews 6:1* is *"Faith toward God"* and not just faith. Faith can be expressed in someone or something other than God. I remember a long while ago while speaking to my manager at work, I was told I was going to be getting a bonus and it was a sum that was unexpected. However, the bonus was still subject to the approval of the company board. Immediately I finished the conversation with my manager, I quickly called my wife and told her what my manager had just told me and without thinking, I started planning how we were going to spend the money and, suddenly, things that had been on the back burner for a while became a priority. As I dropped the phone, I heard the voice of God in my heart saying *"when are you going to start believing my word like that....you have not even received a letter confirming the award and the board has not signed it off."* I had been persuaded that my manager could not lie and that the board was going to sign-off the award.

In this case, what I was hoping for was not even guaranteed. With all the best intentions, the company could have changed the decision to award bonuses due to circumstances beyond their control. It is therefore important to make sure that the *things hoped for* are coming from a more sure source where the intent to give is not governed by external forces that can change.

Let us look at what the prophet Jeremiah had to say about this hope.

> [10] *For thus says the Lord, When seventy years are completed for Babylon, I will visit you and keep My good promise to you, causing you to return to this place.*
> [11] *For I know the thoughts and plans that I have for you, says the Lord, thoughts and plans for welfare and*
> *peace and not for evil, to give you hope in your final outcome.*
> [12] ***Then*** *you will call upon Me, and you will come and pray to Me, and I will hear and heed you.*
> [13] *Then you will seek Me, inquire for, and require Me [as a vital necessity] and find Me when you search for Me with all your heart.*
> [14] *I will be found by you, says the Lord, and I will release you from captivity and gather you from all the nations and all the places to which I have driven you, says the Lord, and I will bring you back to the place from which I caused you to be carried away captive.*
>
> *Jeremiah 29:10-14 (AMP)*

From *verses 11 & 12* we see that without *the things hoped for*, the persuasion of a religious truth or revelation is void. Revelation is only potent when expressed in the direction of a hope. Having hope in your final outcome that comes from God guarantees that He will hear you when you call on Him. Not only is God the giver of the hope, He is also the enduring support that sustains it.

Look at what Jesus taught in *John 15:7-8*

> [7] *If ye abide in me, and my words abide in you, ye shall ask what ye will, and it shall be done unto you.*
> [8] *Herein is my Father glorified, that ye bear much fruit; so shall ye be my disciples.*

> John 15:7-8 (KJV)

> [7] *If you live in Me [abide vitally united to Me] and My words remain in you and continue to live in your hearts, ask whatever you will, and it shall be done for you.*
> [8] *When you bear (produce) much fruit, My Father is honored and glorified, and you show and prove yourselves to be true followers of Mine.*

> John 15:7-8 (AMP)

When the Word of God abides in you and you abide in Him, what you will becomes an expression of His will. God wants His will to be done on earth as it is done in Heaven. Jesus teaches us this in *Matthew 6:9-10*.

> [9] *After this manner therefore pray ye: Our Father which art in heaven, Hallowed be thy name.*
> [10] *Thy kingdom come, Thy will be done in earth, as it is in heaven.*

> Matthew 6:9-10

We cannot hold God to a hope that is not expressed in His will. All the great practitioners of faith, who are examples for us, operated this way. They did not just hope for anything, the *things hoped for* were things that were inspired by God. Given how important *things hoped for* is and considering the fact that almost everything we will achieve in God has to be done this way, a key question that comes to mind is "How do we determine what we hope for?"

Creating "things hoped for"

Hope is usually determined by you having an image of a possible future outcome. This future outcome is, in a lot of cases, subject to forces you may not have control over. To drive this point home, imagine you go to an auction and put in a bid for a particular precious artefact. As soon as your bid is cast, you really don't know if you will get the artefact because someone else may outbid you. However, the image you have in your mind is one of you holding the precious artefact with the emotional satisfaction of being united with the artefact.

As a Christian, this "possible future outcome" is something that should come from the word of God. The process is actually very simple if you know what to do. The starting point is really looking for scriptures that cover the area of you are interested in. So if you have a need around Business, Protection, Intelligence or Health you can start with the scriptures below that cover these four areas:

1.   Business: Power to get wealth

> *[18] But you shall [earnestly] remember the Lord your God, for it is He **who gives you power to get wealth**, that He may establish His covenant which He swore to your fathers, as it is this day.*
>
> *Deuteronomy 8:18 (AMP)*
>
> *[1] Blessed (happy, fortunate, prosperous, and enviable) is the man who walks and lives not in the counsel of the ungodly [following*

their advice, their plans and purposes], nor stands [submissive and inactive] in the path where sinners walk, nor sits down [to relax and rest] where the scornful [and the mockers] gather.

² But his delight and desire are in the law of the Lord, and on His law (the precepts, the instructions, the teachings of God) he habitually meditates (ponders and studies) by day and by night.

³ And he shall be like a tree firmly planted [and tended] by the streams of water, ready to bring forth its fruit in its season; its leaf also shall not fade or wither; and everything he does shall prosper [and come to maturity].

Psalm 1:1-3 (AMP)

2. Protection: Angelic assistance

⁷ A thousand shall fall at thy side, and ten thousand at thy right hand; but it shall not come nigh thee.

⁸ Only with thine eyes shalt thou behold and see the reward of the wicked.

⁹ Because thou hast made the LORD, which is my refuge, even the most High, thy habitation;

¹⁰ There shall no evil befall thee, neither shall any plague come nigh thy dwelling.

¹¹ For he shall give his angels charge over thee, to keep thee in all thy ways.

¹² They shall bear thee up in their hands, lest thou dash thy foot against a stone.

¹³ Thou shalt tread upon the lion and adder: the young lion and the dragon shalt thou trample under

Psalm 91:7-13

3. The Mind: Supernatural mental abilities

⁶ And Elihu the son of Barachel the Buzite answered and said, I am young, and ye are very old; wherefore I was afraid, and durst not shew you mine opinion.

⁷ I said, Days should speak, and multitude of years should teach wisdom.

⁸ But there is a spirit in man: and the inspiration of the Almighty

giveth them understanding.
⁹ Great men are not always wise: neither do the aged understand judgment.
¹⁰ Therefore I said, Hearken to me; I also will shew mine opinion.

Job 32:6-10

⁹⁹ I have more understanding than all my teachers: for thy testimonies are my meditation.
¹⁰⁰ I understand more than the ancients, because I keep thy precepts.

Psalm 119:99-100

³ My words shall be of the uprightness of my heart: and my lips shall utter knowledge clearly.
⁴ The spirit of God hath made me, and the breath of the Almighty hath given me life.

Job 33:3-4

4. Health: Healing

²⁶ And said, If thou wilt diligently hearken to the voice of the LORD thy God, and wilt do that which is right in his sight, and wilt give ear to his commandments, and keep all his statutes, I will put none of these diseases upon thee, which I have brought upon the Egyptians: for I am the LORD that healeth thee.

Exodus 15:26

⁵ But he was wounded for our transgressions, he was bruised for our iniquities: the chastisement of our peace was upon him; and with his stripes we are healed.

Isaiah 53:5

²⁵ His flesh shall be fresher than a child's: he shall return to the days of his youth:

Job 33:25

Starting with these Scriptures has nothing "spiritual" to it. All they do is paint a picture of that "possible future outcome." They are examples of topical Scriptures you can apply the disciplines of prayer, praise, meditation and continuous study of the thoughts expressed in scriptures and any other discipline applicable to you as an individual. The really spiritual and powerful bit happens somewhere in the midst of that process. You hear the voice of God concerning the area of need. The hearing of this voice of God then automatically transmits faith to you.

For many people, as simple as this may sound, defining what you hope for is a challenge. However, we have a classic example in Scriptures that shows us how we can define our hope. Abraham, the father of faith, followed a pattern which could still be applied by anyone who desires to get results by faith. Let us look at this simple process that Abraham followed.

> [21] And being fully persuaded that, what he had promised, he was able also to perform.
> [22] And therefore it was imputed to him for righteousness.
>
> *Romans 4:21-22*

Abraham did not become the father of faith for nothing. There were certain things he did that Heaven recognized as worthy of a response and the honour that was conferred on him. *Verse 21* breaks down the pattern for us.

Firstly, Abraham was fully persuaded concerning what He was hoping for. What is the persuasion, aligned with the Word of God, that is consuming your being? Persuasions are very important because they define the level at which life responds to you and they are largely determined by what you have been exposed to. You cannot be persuaded on a matter beyond the level of information available to you on the matter.

For example, If someone (*an insider*) were to tell you the inside story about meetings that took place before major decisions in governments, most people will talk about those issues more authoritatively than if you did not have that inside information. Partial persuasion means you still have elements of doubt in your heart. These hidden elements are the things that limit the manifestation of the life of God that flows in us. In *Matthew 14:25-32*, Peter walked on water until he *saw* the wind boisterous and Jesus being present did not stop Peter from starting to sink.

> [25] And in the fourth watch of the night Jesus went unto them, walking on the sea.
> [26] And when the disciples saw him walking on the sea, they were troubled, saying, It is a spirit; and they cried out for fear.
> [27] But straightway Jesus spake unto them, saying, Be of good cheer; it is I; be not afraid.
> [28] And Peter answered him and said, Lord, if it be thou, bid me come unto thee on the water.
> [29] And he said, Come. And when Peter was come down out of the ship, he walked on the water, to go to Jesus. [30] But when he saw the wind boisterous, he was afraid; and beginning to sink, he cried, saying, Lord, save me. [31] And immediately Jesus stretched forth his hand, and caught him, and said unto him, O thou of little faith, wherefore didst thou doubt?
> [32] And when they were come into the ship, the wind ceased.

Matthew 14:25-32

This is really amazing. I wonder what would have happened if Peter had not cried out. We need to realise that being in the presence of Jesus without operating the principles of God may not give you the results you deeply desire. This is one reason why some people go to Church regularly without the effect of the God of the Church being visible in their lives.

Secondly, Abraham was not only fully persuaded, He also had an object on which this persuasion was being expressed. He had no cause to doubt the will of God *because the object of his persuasion was something God had promised.* This is one of the most significant areas where the impact of faith is limited. You cannot express your full strength in God while wondering whether the actions you are engaged in are inspired of Him. What God has promised should be more important to you than how He is going to do what He has promised because there may be many routes to the same destination. If you have a satellite navigation system, finding an alternate route is usually just the push of a button away, you can even choose to avoid certain routes.

Lastly, full persuasion is dependent on the ability of God to perform what He has promised. God's ability is unlimited. His ways are past finding out. Though you search from the womb to the grave in old age, He will still remain unfathomable. The Scriptures declare that, *"all things were made by Him and without Him was not anything made that was made."* It does not matter how big your dream is or how insurmountable the challenge may be, it cannot be greater than all he has created. Let us not make a mistake, what we know of creation is not all God has made but all we have discovered. The ability of God is greater than what any mind can fathom. The challenge many people have is that we doubt the authenticity of the Word of God so even when we have Scriptures that deal with the specific areas of life we need help with, we wonder whether God will do what He clearly said in His word that He will do.

Understand your "things hoped for"

By now, we should understand the fact that the image

of things hoped for should be created from the Word of God. As you study the Word of God, the Scriptures will start to connect with the deep desires God has put in your heart. This connection with the Word of God will then start to give meaning and perspective to the experiences in your life and your observations of things that are happening in the lives of others that are relevant to you and your assignment.

A note of caution though, the entrance of the Word of God gives light and there is always the tendency to rush into action. This in itself is not a bad thing but be careful that your level of zeal does not overtake the level of knowledge in you. Pursue images at the level of your persuasion. You may know the final stop of your desires but the next turn is more important than the final stop. You cannot rise to any level of prominence in an area without having a history of associations or and interactions with others in that area. This is usually referred to as industry knowledge. If you are training to be a doctor, it is very likely you will have friends that are doctors with whom you can discuss things specific to that area. The more knowledge you have about an area, the more the persuasion you will express in that area.

The size of what you hope for should determine the level of preparation you are willing to commit to. Any misalignment of this will lead to frustration. If you are planning to be a doctor, at present, there is a minimum of six to seven years of training. It is foolishness to attempt to do it in 6 months.

Chapter 2
THINGS NOT SEEN

We have already dealt with faith being the persuasion of a religious truth or truthfulness of God concerning things hoped for. *Things hoped for* are unseen things as it is not possible to hope for something you are already in possession of. Hope is always linked to an expectation but could also include something you may own but are not necessarily in physical possession of. For example, someone may apply for a job, attend the interview and be offered a role. Even though the physical contract that details the terms of the agreement may not have been signed, a verbal offer may be enough for the applicant to have confidence that the paperwork supporting what has transpired will be made available sometime in the future. At this point, the applicant is no longer "hoping" they get the role. The role was theirs not at the point the agency called to relay information, but at the time the hiring manager decided the candidate that was getting the role.

Faith is the substance of things hoped for. **Faith is also the evidence of things not seen.** Faith is akin to the point at which the hiring manager decides who gets the role. When you say you are operating in faith, you are taking steps being persuaded that a decision has been made in your favour. Faith is what you get as a guarantee that what you are believing for has been granted to you. You always get faith before the manifestation. It is at this point that faith becomes the evidence. The person that possesses faith - the evidence - then starts to take actions that the person without faith may regard as illogical. Faith is the receipt for the down payment you have made toward a desire. A lot of people have problems with faith because they want the receipt without the down payment. Let us now focus on the word "*evidence.*"

When we talk about "*evidence*" we are really talking about proof. It is a series of artefacts that prove something happened. These artefacts could include documents, objects and even the testimony of a witness. The concept of evidence is actually very powerful. The VisualThesaurus gives the following definitions;

♦ *your basis for belief or disbelief; knowledge on which to base belief*

♦ *any factual evidence that helps to establish the truth of something*

♦ *knowledge acquired through study or experience or instruction*

To understand the importance of evidence and the weight it carries in affairs of life, let us look at how a jury uses it. For completeness, let us, again, see how the VisualThesaurus defines what the jury is. It calls it:

a body of citizens sworn to give a true verdict according to the evidence presented in a court of law

This means a jury could give a verdict that will completely change the course of the life of an individual based on evidence (*documents, objects and even the testimony of a witness*) presented to it without being present at the time the event occurred. This means a guilty person could walk free from court as a result of inconclusive evidence. In the same vein, an innocent person could be jailed due to lack of evidence.

Faith is therefore the evidence that challenges of life demand before giving way. It is what the earth demands before it will yield its increase to anyone. *Hebrews 11:6* says, *"But without faith, it is impossible to please Him...."* So the issues of life are wired to look at the level of persuasion in you concerning the thing you are hoping for before responding to you. Faith is about proving the unseen. If the unseen does not exist, there is nothing to prove. Faith is the ticket that allows the believer to prove the unseen.

Motivational speakers tell us that if the level of persuasion you have regarding your desired future is not strong enough, you will not be motivated to action. The things not seen are actually more powerful than the persuasion itself. The things not seen drive the persuasion.

Faith is invisible

We have said the Faith is the persuasion about the things hoped for. It is the evidence of things not seen. If faith is the evidence or proof of the unseen, we need to ask ourselves a very simple question. Is faith visible? Have you ever seen faith? Faith is one of those things in life that we never see but the presence of which can only be shown by something else. Faith cannot be shown in isolation. For example;

♦ *We breathe air but cannot see air*

♦ *We feel the wind but do not see the wind*

♦ *Approval is not something you see. It is demonstrated through other means e.g. a letter of approval, a nod or the stretching of the sceptre in your direction if we borrow a leaf from some of the kings in the Old Testament*

♦ *Love is not something you see. It is something you feel*

Faith is something you reach a conclusion on based on other factors. How then can we see faith? How can we determine that faith exists? I believe there are two primary ways the presence of faith can be confirmed.

1. Faith by Words

> *[13] We having the same spirit of faith, according as it is written, I believed, and therefore have I spoken; we also believe, and therefore speak;*
>
> *2 Corinthians 4:13*

What you say with your mouth is taken as evidence of what you believe. This is why the Bible declares in *Proverbs 18:21* that *"Death and life are in the power of the tongue: and they that love it shall eat the fruit thereof."* A person can believe in God with their whole heart but never present the evidence.

> *[10] For with the heart man believeth unto righteousness; and with the mouth confession is made unto salvation.*
>
> *Romans 10:10*

Let me explain this. To get born-again, you heard the message of the gospel of salvation, believed the facts or evidence presented to you, just like a jury would have done, and reached the level of persuasion to bring you to the place of confession that indeed Jesus not only died for the sin of humanity, he died for your sin.

Did you notice in *Romans 10:10* that believing only brings you into the right relationship with God but it is actually what you confess that brings salvation. Even devils believe. Many people may miss the best God has for them not because they did not believe but because they did not say with their mouth what they believed.

With the mouth confession is made unto salvation. If your heart believes it but your mouth does not confess it, the power to create will not be released. On the other hand, if your mouth is consistently speaking what your heart does not believe, your confession will re-programme your heart to believe what your mouth is saying. If your mouth then constantly speaks negative things that you do not really desire, the negative confessions will create a world of frustrating experiences around you.

2. Faith by Works

Another way the Bible tells us we can see faith is by works. The level of results you command is proportional to the level of persuasion in your heart.

14 What doth it profit, my brethren, though a man say he hath faith, and have not works? can faith save him?
15 If a brother or sister be naked, and destitute of daily food,
16 And one of you say unto them, Depart in peace, be ye warmed and filled; notwithstanding ye give them not those things which are needful to the body; what doth it profit?
17 Even so faith, if it hath not works, is dead, being alone.

James 2:14-17

If there is no physical manifestation of something tangible that you got by the principle of faith, there is no way we can know you have faith. Faith without works is dead. There is no point jumping up and shouting, "*I've got faith.*" Faith is not really the end result of what you want. Your *things hoped for* or your desire is really what you are after. Faith is only the down payment. Once you have the down payment, you must produce it at the point of exchange. In some retail stores, they provide stands where you can view the products you want and pay for them. Once you have paid, you get given a receipt with an *order number* on it. This receipt is then presented at a counter when the *order number* is called. If the receipt holder does not turn up with the receipt, the ordered item is put aside till later.

[17] *Even so faith, if it hath not works, is dead, being alone.*

James 2:17

I believe many miss out simply because they did not present their receipt at the point of collection. They try to make payments at the point of collection. You need to present your receipt to obtain your desire. The level of works is the thermometer for faith. When works don't follow faith, it means the holder of the evidence is doubting the authenticity of the evidence. This means the evidence that confirms the unseen has not really been fully received.

When faith came

Faith is something every Christian cannot do without. Without faith the Christian cannot please God (*Hebrews*

11:6), without faith, a person cannot even be saved (Ephesians 2:8). If these facts are true, one of the critical questions we should ask ourselves is this; when exactly do we acquire faith? Is faith a tangible substance that gets deposited in us or is it something we already possess?

Many times, we quote *Romans 12 :3* which says;

> *3 For I say, through the grace given unto me, to every man that is among you, not to think of himself more highly than he ought to think; but to think soberly, according as God hath dealt to every man the measure of faith.*
>
> *Romans 12 :3*

Many people quote this scripture and use it to justify the fact that everybody has got faith. While I do not particularly dispute that thought as being the case, if we read the preceding verses and the subsequent verses, there is a conclusion we could come to that is often missed.

Let us read from *verses 1 to 6* so we can see the full context in which Apostle Paul was having this conversation.

> *1 I beseech you therefore, brethren, by the mercies of God, that ye present your bodies a living sacrifice, holy, acceptable unto God, which is your reasonable service.*
> *2 And be not conformed to this world: but be ye transformed by the renewing of your mind, that ye may prove what is that good, and acceptable, and perfect, will of God.*
> *3 For I say, through the grace given unto me, to every man that is among you, not to think of himself more highly than he ought to think; but to think soberly, according as God hath dealt to every man the measure of faith.*
> *4 For as we have many members in one body, and all members have not the same office:*
> *5 So we, being many, are one body in Christ, and every one members one of another.*

⁶ Having then gifts differing according to the grace that is given to us, whether prophecy, let us prophesy according to the proportion of faith;

Romans 12:1-6

The Apostle starts by pointing out what he considers to be our reasonable service to God and what we can do; firstly, to avoid conformity with the world and secondly prove that the will of God exists and was relevant to the people he was addressing. If there was no *"will of God"* accessible to the people, encouraging them to prove it would have made no sense. So as Christians, we have a responsibility, like the jury in a court of law, to prove (*test and certify reputable*) that a living God exists behind the written and physical artefacts of Scriptures that we have with us. Remember, there is no way we can test and certify something without having the results to show. The only way to *"prove"* the will of God is to show the results of faith. In *Hebrews 11:3*, the Bible tells us that faith was what the elders used to obtain a good report.

Paul then sounds a note of warning – think soberly - as it appeared some were beginning to think about themselves higher than they should have been. Thinking you are the CEO of your organisation does not mean you can start acting like the CEO of the organisation. There is a process between having an idea and having the substance of the idea. As I always say, there is a difference between a woman conceiving and the same woman delivering a baby. To start having labour pains at conception is not normal. Keep the thoughts in your head until the opportunity for promotion to CEO presents itself to you. The breaking of the water and the contractions is what signals the baby's time to come out is due. In the same way, your thoughts and actions about greatness

~ 20 ~

need to be consistent with the timing of God. Babies do not determine when they come out of the womb, circumstances that surround them do. Trying to come out before your time could mean you come out pre-mature reducing your likelihood of survival.

Paul did not just say, *"God has dealt to every man the measure of faith"*, but he was linking the thought patterns in the mind with the measure of faith that God had given every person. In essence, the thinking of every Christian should be regulated by the revelation of the Word of God they have. Revelation or insight into the Word of God is the signal from heaven that you have the authorisation to proceed with the thoughts and actions that the revelation dictates. Faith starts where the will of God is known. This is the point where the seed of faith is deposited concerning a desire. It is however *"dead"* at this point because there are no works associated with it. Remember what the Bible says in James.

> *[17] Even so **faith, if it hath not works, is dead**, being alone.*
>
> *James 2:17*

So, the revelation is not faith, works alone is not faith. Faith is when action is taken based on the demands and instructions given through revelation. So revelation not acted upon will not produce the desired result.

Look at the example of Jesus. He followed a similar pattern. He only did what He saw the Father do. The works of the Father guided his actions. The Gospel of John tells the story of a man Jesus healed on the Sabbath that caused the Jews to rise up against Him.

> *[14] Afterward Jesus findeth him in the temple, and said unto him, Behold, thou art made whole: sin no more, lest a worse thing come*

unto thee.

¹⁵ The man departed, and told the Jews that it was Jesus, which had made him whole.

¹⁶ And therefore did the Jews persecute Jesus, and sought to slay him, because he had done these things on the sabbath day.

¹⁷ But Jesus answered them, My Father worketh hitherto, and I work.

¹⁸ Therefore the Jews sought the more to kill him, because he not only had broken the sabbath, but said also that God was his Father, making himself equal with God.

¹⁹ Then answered Jesus and said unto them, Verily, verily, I say unto you, The Son can do nothing of himself, but what he seeth the Father do: for what things soever he doeth, these also doeth the Son likewise.

²⁰ For the Father loveth the Son, and sheweth him all things that himself doeth: and he will shew him greater works than these, that ye may marvel.

²¹ For as the Father raiseth up the dead, and quickeneth them; even so the Son quickeneth whom he will.

John 5:19-21

Look at *verse 20*, Jesus did what the Father had shown Him. What is God showing you and what are you doing about what He has shown you? The actions you take in line with what He has shown you is what demonstrates your faith. This story is really very profound. Many people have been limited by limitations simply because they are not acting on what God has shown them. They have allowed people to use the letter of the Word to limit them. The Jews were more concerned about the law of the Sabbath that was broken that they failed to realise that a man who had had an infirmity for thirty-eight years had just been supernaturally healed.

When you start following this principle of faith, you will start breaking the limitations that men want to impose on you. When they say there is a casting down, you will be saying that there is a lifting up. It is, of course, important that we acknowledge the signposts God has placed along the path to lead up to the point where we see the things of the Father clearly.

In *Galatians 3:23*, Apostle Paul makes a very striking statement. He says, "*...but before faith came we were kept under the law....*" The presence of these limitation in our lives is an indication that we have not seen clearly the way of escape that God would have taken to navigate through the challenges.

> [22] *But the scripture hath concluded all under sin, that the promise by faith of Jesus Christ might be given to them that believe.*
> [23] *But before faith came, we were kept under the law, shut up unto the faith which should afterwards be revealed.*
> [24] *Wherefore the law was our schoolmaster to bring us unto Christ, that we might be justified by faith.*
> [25] *But after that faith is come, we are no longer under a schoolmaster.*
>
> *Galatians 3:22-25*

Paul was quite clear in his comments, once faith came, the power of the schoolmaster of life could not hold us down. We are able to mount up wings as eagles and soar over the challenges of life.

Chapter 3

A CHANNEL OF DISCOVERY

*[1]Now faith is the substance of things hoped for, the evidence of
things not seen.*
[2] For by it the elders obtained a good report.
*[3] Through faith we understand that the worlds were framed by the
word of God, so that things which are seen were not made of things
which do appear.*

Hebrews 11:1-3

This whole chapter of Hebrews is probably the
most concentrated chapter on the subject of faith
in the Bible. The chapter does not only give
us definitions of faith, it highlights the benefits that
accrued to those who were practitioners of faith.

From *verse 1* we see two definitions of faith.

◆ Faith is the substance of things hoped for.

◆ Faith is the evidence of things not seen.

Remember the word "faith" really means *"persuasion
of religious truth or the truthfulness of God"* while
"substance" denotes *"having something set under"*
or *"having support to stand or lean on."* This means
when the writer of Hebrews tells us that "faith is the
substance of things hoped for", the writer is making us
understand that;

Faith is having a persuasion of a religious truth (or
revelation as we call it these days) concerning what we
are hoping for while having something as a support to

lean on.

Looking carefully at *verse 2*, it appears as though faith is depicted as a tool, something the elders used in exchange for what we could describe as another product called *"a good report"* while in *verse 3*, faith is depicted as a *channel* through which understanding comes. The ability to separate these two thoughts i.e. *Faith as a tool* and *Faith as a channel*, like the writer intended and thus wrote, is what makes the difference between a satisfied practitioner of faith and a frustrated one. Without understanding this two aspects of faith, the reality of what Christ has done for us as believers can be an elusive dream. You cannot use *Faith as a channel* when faith needs to be used as a tool and vice-versa.

Faith as a channel therefore deals with gaining intelligence from a supernatural source while *Faith as a tool* deals with using the intelligence gained effectively. *Faith as a channel* deals with discoveries from Scriptures while *Faith as a tool* deals with actions that are aligned with the discoveries made. *Faith as a channel* is passive, *Faith as a tool* is active. In *Faith as a channel*, you are waiting on God, in *Faith as a tool*, God is waiting on you. *Faith as a channel* deals with conception, *Faith as a tool* deals with delivery. No matter how smooth the delivery process, a pregnant woman cannot mistaken conception for delivery.

Why is faith important when you are looking for insight into the word of God?

- ♦ You are attempting to gain understanding from a God you cannot see

- ♦ You are using Scriptures compiled by people you

have never met

♦ You probably have never engaged in a natural process to validate that the scriptures are indeed authentic. It is something you believe

♦ You have to rely on an internal witness to believe that the voice you hear is really God

All these four points have a big statement that could very easily just replace them all. BELIEVING IN THE UNSEEN.

This concept of *Faith as a channel* and *Faith as a tool* presented in *verses 2 & 3* actually help give more meaning to *verse 1*. "Faith is the evidence of things not seen" implies that for faith to exist, *things not seen* must exist. You cannot have evidence of something that does not exist or something that did not happen. Of course, I am assuming that evidence has not been fabricated for gain as in the case of Stephen in *Acts 6:13* where false witnesses were set up. If you find "things not seen", faith, *the necessary inward conviction* that will enable you use what you have found as a tool will be present. A workman with a tool he does not know how to use has the same level of productivity as a workman with the knowledge on how to use the tool but without the tool. Understanding (*instructions and thoughts that register with your senses*) not applied does not produce a good report.

If you go into a supermarket and you want to buy something that is age restricted, you may have to present evidence of your age. In this situation, the shopper is relying on the result of *a verification process* to determine whether you qualify for what you want to buy or not. The result of that *verification process* is the pass you require for purchase. When you have the result of the *verification process*, you can make the demand for your desire. This verification process is what *Faith as a Channel* is all about.

As I said before, trying to come out before your time could mean you come out premature reducing your likelihood of survival. Attempting to use faith as a tool before using it as a channel is like having a premature baby. Using faith as a tool is dependent on whether or not you had used it as a channel. There is no great practitioner of faith that is not *seeing* things spiritually. One of the greatest challenges of faith practitioners is understanding that faith is not an isolated spiritual substance. Faith cannot be present if *"things not seen"* does not exist. Faith can also not be absent if *"things not seen"* is present. Both go hand in hand.

You cannot use faith as a tool without a set of instructions or thoughts registering with your mind that an invisible substance without earthly form exists. This is where many people miss the principle of faith. Faith does not create the unseen, it is the *evidence* that the unseen exists. The unseen is not something you create, it is something you become aware of. *Faith is the evidence of things not seen.* Faith is the tool that makes the unseen seen. Faith does not call things that don't exist spiritually as though they do. Faith calls things that exist spiritually as though they exist physically.

When we talk about *"evidence"* we are really talking about proof. Remember, we said in an earlier chapter that *"evidence"* is really a series of artefacts (*documents, objects and even the testimony of a witness*) that *prove something happened.* Nobody asks for evidence of events that have not happened unless they are trying to predict the future but no jury can judge the future.

We described evidence as:

♦ your basis for belief or disbelief; knowledge on which to base belief

♦ any factual evidence that helps to establish the truth of something

♦ knowledge acquired through study or experience or instruction

The evidence you have available to you is what gives you the confidence in the affairs of life. The issues of life are wired to look at the level of persuasion you have in the evidence of the unseen you are aware of before responding to you. Faith is about proving the unseen. If the unseen does not exist, there is nothing to prove.

Before we go on, it is important that we remind ourselves of the fundamental *understanding* that the writer refers to in *verse 3*. What was the understanding that came through faith? It is the understanding that it is the Word of God that gave the world a physical form and that what you see is as a result of what you don't see. The world which is seen was created by words which are unseen. J.B Phillips in his New Testament translation of these verses refers to *"principles which are invisible."*

11 *1-3* *Now faith means putting our full confidence in the things we hope for, it means being certain of things we cannot see. It was this kind of faith that won their reputation for the saints of old. And it is after all only by faith that our minds accept as fact that the whole scheme of time and space was created by God's*

command—that the world which we can see has come into being through principles which are invisible.

Hebrews 11:1-3 (PHILLIPS)

In other words, there are invisible elements that govern what we see. Buildings don't just emerge from nowhere, they are the product of invisible ideas in the minds of men. So there are people who have ideas yet are outwardly unproductive but I am yet to meet someone that is outwardly productive that does not have a mind filled with insight.

Chapter 4
UNDERSTANDING FAITH AS A CHANNEL

As I mentioned, Faith as a channel is about discoveries. You cannot operate in faith effectively if you have not made discoveries from the Scriptures. When you use faith as a channel, you are expecting to connect with the mind of God. The thoughts of God which were not your thoughts become your thoughts and creates a union with divinity. The mysteries which had been hidden from ages become revealed to you. The Scriptures which in *Matthew 13:11* says, "*...it is given unto you to know the mysteries of the kingdom of heaven, but to them it is not given*" becomes a reality in your life in the area of your have deepest thirst.

The word *"know"* is translated in different ways in Scriptures. The word translated here was *"Ginosko."* *Matthew 13:11* would have read, "*... it is given unto you to "Ginosko" the mysteries.....*" The Strong's Concordance defines *"Ginosko"* as encompassing the following, "*to learn to know, come to know, get a knowledge or perceive, feel to become known, have knowledge of, to understand, to speak, be aware.*"

"Learning to know" gives the impression of someone learning a new language. In learning languages, you need to learn a lot more than just the words. The pronunciation and the way words are combined is also important. Pronouncing a word wrongly may give you away as a non-native speaker of the language.

The Mariam-Webster dictionary defines language as, *"the words, their pronunciation and the methods of combining them used and understood by a community"* while the Visual Thesaurus also defines it as *the cognitive processes involved in producing and understanding linguistic communication.* For example, *"he did not have the language to express his feelings."* So the feelings and emotions are real, the desire to express the feelings and emotions are real but the words, the methods of combining them to demonstrate that you are a member of the community is what is lacking. It is this gap that *"Ginosko"* plugs.

"Ginosko" gives you knowledge that is consistent with what anyone in the community of Heaven will say if asked about the knowledge you have received. *"Ginosko"* brings a consistency between your language and the language of Heaven. In *Daniel 10:11*, the angel said to Daniel, *"....O Daniel,...understand the words that I speak unto thee...for unto thee am I now sent..."*. The understanding Daniel had was the same understanding Heaven was bringing to him. In other words, his interpretation of the words were the same as that of Heaven after the Angel gave him the understanding.

"Ginosko" deals with absolute knowledge. Knowledge that is revealed from God. Elihu, in *Job, 37:16* refers to this type of knowledge as "perfected knowledge." For example, Jesus, in *Matthew 16:17*, told Peter, *"... flesh and blood hath not revealed it unto thee, but my father which is in Heaven."* implying that there was a body of knowledge Peter had come into an understanding of, but what exactly was it the Father revealed to Peter? God revealed (*Greek: Apokalupto:- to uncover, lay open what has been veiled or covered up, disclose, make bare, to make known, make manifest*) to him that Jesus was the Christ, the son of

the living God. This knowledge is the exact knowledge that Heaven had regarding the identity of Christ. There is no way you can take away or add to this knowledge without altering the context of the revelation.

There are a few concepts we need to pull out from what Jesus said to Peter here to help us build a right foundation for understanding *Faith as a Channel* because the kind of knowledge Peter *"came to know"* here is the end result of using Faith as a Channel.

1. *God can bring knowledge directly to you*

You can come into an awareness of knowledge directly from God without conferring with any earthly source. Apostle Paul in *1 Corinthians 11:23* says, *"For I have received of the Lord that which also I delivered unto you......"* In the book of *Revelation 1:1*, the description is even more graphic. Let us look at how the Amplified Bible translates it.

> [1] *[This is] the revelation of Jesus Christ [His unveiling of the divine mysteries]. God gave it to Him to disclose and make known to His bond servants certain things which must shortly and speedily come to pass in their entirety. And He sent and communicated it through His angel (messenger) to His bond servant John,*
>
> Revelation 1:1 (AMP)

God the Father is the custodian of these mysteries so you can see why Jesus said, *"My Father in Heaven..."* and why getting any form of revelation from Scriptures is the Father moving on your behalf.

2. *Godly knowledge can come from natural sources*

"Flesh and Blood", in this case, natural sources, can give you knowledge. In *Matthew 16:13*, when Jesus asked his disciples the question, *"Whom do men say that I the Son of man am?"*, we get a flavour of what can happen if we rely on men. *"And they said, Some say that thou art John the Baptist: some, Elias; and others, Jeremias, or one of the prophets."* Knowledge you get from *"Flesh and Blood"* is not necessarily wrong, it just needs to be judged against what is in you. The answer to the confusion that exists externally is to discover the internal answer in you. Who do **you** say God is?

Your answer to this question is predicated on what discoveries you have made. If you have not used your faith as a channel, you will only see God as men have described Him to you but when you find Him through your personal search, you will discover that He is greater than any description any man has ever given you. Abraham, Isaac and Jacob, as great as these men were, only knew God by the name *"God Almighty."* The name Jehovah is not a name either of these men would have used to describe God (*Exodus 6:3*). Their discoveries of God had not uncovered "Jehovah."

We walk by faith and not be sight because you cannot use the finite to describe the infinite. There is no language on earth with sufficient vocabulary to describe God. *Job 36:26* says, *"… God is great and we know Him not, neither can the number of His years be searched out."* Eternity is an unsearchable space. The quicker we rely on our discoveries from Scriptures the better for humanity.

3. *You may need help to understand knowledge*

You can be unaware of the revelation of God through you. If Jesus had not spoken, Peter may not have realised that *"My Father in Heaven"* was speaking through him. The identification of the revelation of God to you can be validated by someone else.

The knowledge imparted to Peter came from God and not Jesus even though Jesus confirmed it. In other words, you can receive revelation from Heaven that does not necessarily come from the person God has placed over you. However, the person God has placed over you should be able to help you rightly identify God in your actions. Remember the story of Samuel and Eli?

Faith as a Channel

Let us look at excerpts of the parable of the sower in *Matthew 13* to get a better understanding of what I call Faith as a Channel.

¹ The same day went Jesus out of the house, and sat by the sea side.
² And great multitudes were gathered together unto him, so that he went into a ship, and sat; and the whole multitude stood on the shore.
³ And he spake many things unto them in parables, saying, Behold, a sower went forth to sow;

Matthew 13:1-3

⁹ Who hath ears to hear, let him hear.
¹⁰ And the disciples came, and said unto him, Why speakest thou

unto them in parables?

11 He answered and said unto them, Because it is given unto you to know the mysteries of the kingdom of heaven, but to them it is not given.

12 For whosoever hath, to him shall be given, and he shall have more abundance: but whosoever hath not, from him shall be taken away even that he hath.

13 Therefore speak I to them in parables: because they seeing see not; and hearing they hear not, neither do they understand.

14 And in them is fulfilled the prophecy of Esaias, which saith, By hearing ye shall hear, and shall not understand; and seeing ye shall see, and shall not perceive:

15 For this people's heart is waxed gross, and their ears are dull of hearing, and their eyes they have closed; lest at any time they should see with their eyes and hear with their ears, and should understand with their heart, and should be converted, and I should heal them.

16 But blessed are your eyes, for they see: and your ears, for they hear.

17 For verily I say unto you, That many prophets and righteous men have desired to see those things which ye see, and have not seen them; and to hear those things which ye hear, and have not heard them.

18 Hear ye therefore the parable of the sower.

Matthew 13:1-3, 9-18

Many people are still hearing the Word of God in parables. Though they stand in the presence of divinity and hear the Word of God yet they do not have the understanding that creates belief in the heart. You cannot have faith if you do not believe and you cannot believe if Scriptures are not opened to you (*Romans 10*). This concept of understanding of parables is one of the greatest foundational truths that Christians today need to understand.

A closer look at *verse 15* explains why faith needs to be used as a channel. Through the fall of Adam and Eve, man is inherently in a place where:

15 For this people's heart is waxed gross, and their ears are dull of hearing, and their eyes they have closed; lest at any time they should

see with their eyes and hear with their ears, and should understand
with their heart, and should be converted, and I should heal them.

Matthew 13:15

The very channels that are required for making discoveries from Scriptures have all been blocked. The heart is waxed gross, the ears are dull of hearing and the eyes are closed. The heart, the processing unit for discoveries, has been left untouched for so long that an overhaul is required for it to function properly. From, *Romans 10:10*, we understand that *"with the heart man believeth unto righteousness."* *Job 38:36* says, *"...God has given understanding to the heart."* So we don't believe with the eyes or the ears, we believe with the heart but the eyes and the ears are the gate to the heart. Without believing in the heart, a right relationship with God cannot be contemplated.

In what Jesus describes here though, the ears have heard the same thing over and over without the required intervention of the supernatural and has lost the ability the pick up the distinct nature of sound. Dull does not mean you don't hear, you just don't hear the distinctions in the sounds you hear and therefore loose the intelligence the sound is giving you. Elijah the prophet, in *1 King 18:41* said, *"...there is the sound of the abundance of rain."* Sound is a function of the ears. Clearly, there was no cloud at this time so Elijah could not have been looking at the physical circumstances to reach the conclusion that there was a sound indicating rain was about to fall. There is a sound made in the spirit ever before the clouds start to gather in the skies. Movements in the spirit create sounds that only the sensitive ear can pick up. In *Genesis 3:8*, Adam and Eve *"heard the voice of the LORD God walking."* The **walking** of God was reaching Adam and Eve as the voice of the Lord. They heard His voice from His movements.

It is the hearing of these movements that bring you into the fold of God and differentiates you in the affairs of life. See what Jesus said in *John 10:16*, "*And other sheep I have, which are not of this fold: them also I must bring, and they shall hear my voice; and there shall be one fold, and one shepherd.*"

The eye is actually an important channel here, In *Matthew 6:22*, Jesus paints a very significant picture that we should consider.

> *[19] Lay not up for yourselves treasures upon earth, where moth and rust doth corrupt, and where thieves break through and steal:*
> *[20] But lay up for yourselves treasures in heaven, where neither moth nor rust doth corrupt, and where thieves do not break through nor steal:*
> *[21] For where your treasure is, there will your heart be also.*
> *[22] The light of the body is the eye: if therefore thine eye be single, thy whole body shall be full of light.*
> *[23] But if thine eye be evil, thy whole body shall be full of darkness. If therefore the light that is in thee be darkness, how great is that darkness!*

Matthew 6:19-23

The eye is called the light of the body. Without light the heart cannot function rightly. It will be like the engine of a car that has no spark plugs. The engine is capable of pulling the mass of the car but cannot because there is no spark to cause the combustion that generates the force to crank the engine.

If you are in this state that *verse 15* describes, you will have the actions of religion but not the power of Christianity. On reading *verse 11*, you would have thought that the disciples were in that place where they understood the parable and were just wondering why Jesus was not explaining the "real meaning" or "revelation," as we call it today, to the people who were listening to Him.

However, *verse 18* paints a different picture. Look at what it says again, *"Hear ye therefore the parable of the sower"* This statement from Jesus indicates that even the disciples did not understand the story. Why would Jesus have had to explain it again if they already had the understanding of the parable?

Many people are hearing God like the people did in *verse 3* but *Faith as a Channel* is what gives you what Jesus gave the disciples in *verse 18*. God fills you to the degree of your thirst and your thirst is evidenced by the questions you ask. A Scripture you do not place a demand on does not automatically produce results in your life. This is why many people associated with Scriptures but do not have the experience of God in their lives.

If faith is not used a channel, you cannot use faith as a tool. I have said this many times. Faith does not just come from hearing the Word of God, faith comes from hearing God speak. Faith, as we know it, came by Abraham hearing God. No man of God should be a substitute for God in your life. Even Jesus, in His capacity as man, came to show us the Father.

Your ears hear after your eyes see

You need to see with your eyes otherwise you will not hear and believe God. This is why using faith as a channel is extremely important. If a picture has not formed in your mind, information relevant to the achievement of the picture will be ignored by you. Your mind only attracts information it considers valuable. The way the mind makes that judgement call of what is valuable is to link events around you to a goal (*a picture of a future state you desire*) you have.

Look at *verse 15* again. It explains why faith needs to be used as a channel.

> [15] *For this people's heart is waxed gross, and their ears are dull of hearing, and their eyes they have closed; lest at any time they should see with their eyes and hear with their ears, and should understand with their heart, and should be converted, and I should heal them.*

Matthew 13:15

Did you notice that the seeing comes before the hearing? Look at the hierarchy in the statement.

- *...they should SEE with their eyes...*

- *...and HEAR with their ears...*

- *...should UNDERSTAND with their heart...*

- *...be CONVERTED (This is where the mind gets expanded. Romans 12:1-2)*

- *...I should HEAL them...*

If you don't see yourself in a place where you already have what you are believing God for, you will not attract the relevant information through hearing preachers and teachers that will help you take the unseen and make it seen. You will walk past the provision God has made for you.

While it is not impossible to *just get healed*, it is much more difficult to maintain your healing without "catching" a revelation about healing. This is the seeing part. To be healed, you need more than just seeing. You need to hear and understand and be converted. If you do not change your mind to confirm with what you are hearing, you will have a challenge proving the will of God.

Applying the Word of God is a repeatable process that guarantees a successful outcome every time. It works when you are thrown in the lions den; it also works when you are bound and dropped in the fire; it works when you have a wedding and run out of wine; it works when you need to feed five thousand men and you only have five loaves of bread and two fishes; it even still works when a body has been dead for four days and put in a tomb.

For those of you close to me, you would have heard this story many times but it is important that I tell it again here so you can see the story of someone who did not walk past the provision God had made.

I was in the organiser's room of a singles conference a while ago and the book "*Piercing the Spirit of the Sadducees*" had just been released and I was still reeling from the revelation God gave in that book when this lady walks up to me and says, "*there is something on you, I don't know what it is but I need it.*" Initially, I was taken aback but on second thoughts, I realised that the statement was loaded and there were lessons to be learnt from the experience. Look at the thoughts I took from her statement.

1. You can "see" the anointing on someone

She identified that there was "*something*" on me. How she did this, I have no idea but I know there is an inner witness in everybody that leads you to recognising God in others. One of the four discoveries T. L Osborn made in the early days of his ministry was "*God in another man.*" Many people remain frustrated in life because they do not recognise God in other people. There are many things God wants to bring to you that he never does directly. He comes through other people. The good news is that you never know who or when you will come in contact with these people and therefore have to continue to love and respect others so you don't close doors that should be open.

2. *The anointing can be transferred*

She understood the fact that the anointing could be transferred. She would not have asked for it if she had not come into an understanding of the fact that the anointing could be transferred in answer to the discoveries you have made in the secret place. One thing many miss here is that they do not recognise that the anointing only operates like it did in this case in answer to the purposes and plans of God.

Many have had hands laid on them to no effect. They have desired the anointing on this person and that person but in *1 Samuel 10:1*, Samuel anoints Saul saying, *"Is it not because the Lord hath anointed thee to be captain over his inheritance?"* The only reason the anointing could rest on Saul was because *"...the Lord HATH anointed..."* No external anointing can trigger results where internal discoveries have not been made. Again, in *Acts 19:11-12*, God wrought special miracles by the hands of Paul, so that from his body were brought unto the sick handkerchiefs or aprons, and the diseases departed from them, and the evil spirits went out of them. The anointing is transferable but it is people without discoveries that remain fruitless.

3. She overcame her personal fears

This lady was not the only one in the room yet she did not hesitate to go after what she needed. What if I responded negatively? What if she made a fool of herself in the presence of the other people in the room? What if I responded like Jesus did to the Sy-rophe-nici-an woman? For every faith story you come across, the possibility of nothing happening a result of the action was very present.

I believe there is a certain amount of fear we need to overcome before touching the things of God. Look at the number of times Jesus said *"Fear not"* in the gospel. Faith just delivers irrespective of physical reality. Even though I was in the same meeting room with this lady, she could have kept quiet and would have missed a great opportunity to become an author. The discoveries you make always attract the necessary resources to help make your dreams come to pass.

4. She did not despise the method

Interestingly, all I did was to give her a handshake. There was no preaching or lengthy prayer. Yet, about a month last when I saw her, she said to me, *"Since the day I shook you hand, I have not stopped writing"* and she had produced the manuscript of the thoughts that had been going through her mind. That manuscript became a very powerful book called *"Who Am I?"* Is it everybody I give a handshake that becomes an author? Of course not. However, everybody with a discovery that places a demand on the anointing receives an answer.

She did not despise the method of transfer. Some people would have asked, "A handshake? Is that's all?" Is that not what Naaman asked in 2 *Kings 5:10-13.*

> [10] *And Elisha sent a messenger unto him, saying, Go and wash in Jordan seven times, and thy flesh shall come again to thee, and thou shalt be clean.*
> [11] *But Naaman was wroth, and went away, and said, Behold, I thought, He will surely come out to me, and stand, and call on the name of the LORD his God, and strike his hand over the place, and recover the leper.* [12] *Are not Abana and Pharpar, rivers of Damascus, better than all the waters of Israel? may I not wash in them, and be clean? So he turned and went away in a rage.*
> [13] *And his servants came near, and spake unto him, and said, My father, if the prophet had bid thee do some great thing, wouldest thou not have done it? how much rather then, when he saith to thee, Wash, and be clean?*

2 Kings 5:10-13

Don't miss out on God's blessing because you either do not like the vessel or the method through which God comes. Remember, He could also speak through animals.

Take the information I have given you here and start using your faith as a channel of discovery and watch the amazing results that will break out in your daily life.

Chapter 5

WHAT ABRAHAM FOUND?

A braham, the father of faith, used faith as a channel. He relied on discoveries he had made concerning God. Apostle Paul explains what Abraham did in *Romans 4*.

Look at the Apostle's question?

> ¹ *What shall we say then that Abraham our father, as pertaining to the flesh, hath found?*
>
> *Romans 4:1*

In order to get a *"Matthew 18"* experience, I looked at the word *"found"* in the literal greek using the Strong's Online Concordance. The word translated was a word called *"hyoo-ris'-ko."* It means:

1. *to come upon, hit upon, to meet with:*
   a. *after searching, to find a thing sought ,*
   b. *without previous search, to find (by chance), to fall in with,*
   c. *those who come or return to a place*

2. *to find by enquiry, thought, examination, scrutiny, observation, to find out by practice and experience*
   a. *to see, learn, discover, understand ,*
   b. *to be found i.e. to be seen, be present,*

c. to be discovered, recognised, detected, to show one's self out, of one's character or state as found out by others (men, God, or both)

d. to get knowledge of, come to know, God

3. to find out for one's self, to acquire, get, obtain, procure

From these definitions, we can see that Abraham personally searched things out by *enquiry, thought, examination, observation, practice and experience*. He found out things himself. He did not rely on the discoveries of others where the important things of the unseen were concerned. *Hebrews 11:8-10* gives us an idea of what his searching experience was like.

> [8] *By faith Abraham, when he was called to go out into a place which he should after receive for an inheritance, obeyed; and he went out, not knowing whither he went.*
> [9] *By faith he sojourned in the land of promise, as in a strange country, dwelling in tabernacles with Isaac and Jacob, the heirs with him of the same promise:*
> [10] *For he looked for a city which hath foundations, whose builder and maker is God.*
>
> *Hebrews 11:8-10*

Like Abraham, you also should be looking for a city whose builder and maker is God. What we are doing with books today was a city I found. After much crying in my bed in the night time, with deep thoughts going through my mind, I would wake up in the morning and start praying in the tongues, listen to everything I could find on faith from everyone I knew was an authority on the subject until suddenly, I found something and the word of the Lord came to me saying, "*Remember the vision I gave you? Go and write it in a book.*" This was not a revelation, it was an instruction. We will talk a bit more about this later because a lot of people move on revelation rather than instruction. I strongly believe there is a pattern in scriptures to follow. A pattern that takes us *from revelation to instruction to actions culminating in faith based results.*

Abraham dwelled in tabernacles with his son and grandson while looking for a city that had foundations with God as the builder and maker. Many want to operate the faith of Abraham without the discoveries of Abraham. *Romans 4:12* talks about those *"...who also walk in the steps of THAT FAITH of our father Abraham, which he had being yet uncircumcised."* No wonder many are frustrated in their efforts. Faith comes through your personal relationship with God.

What did Abraham find?

The fact that we are still talking about Abraham today and claiming his blessings is testament to the potency of what he found. Let us look at what the Bible tells us he found in Paul's epistle to the Roman Church.

> [21] *But now the righteousness of God without the law is manifested, being witnessed by the law and the prophets;*
> [22] *Even the righteousness of God which is by faith of Jesus Christ unto all and upon all them that believe: for there is no difference:*
> [23] *For all have sinned, and come short of the glory of God;*
> [24] *Being justified freely by his grace through the redemption that is in Christ Jesus:*
> [25] *Whom God hath set forth to be a propitiation through faith in his blood, to declare his righteousness for the remission of sins that are past, through the forbearance of God;*
> [26] *To declare, I say, at this time his righteousness: that he might be just, and the justifier of him which believeth in Jesus.*
> [27] *Where is boasting then? It is excluded. By what law? of works? Nay: but by the law of faith.*

²⁸ Therefore we conclude that a man is justified by faith without the deeds of the law.
²⁹ Is he the God of the Jews only? is he not also of the Gentiles? Yes, of the Gentiles also:
³⁰ Seeing it is one God, which shall justify the circumcision by faith, and uncircumcision through faith.
³¹ Do we then make void the law through faith? God forbid: yea, we establish the law.
¹ What shall we say then that Abraham our father, as pertaining to the flesh, hath found?
² For if Abraham were justified by works, he hath whereof to glory; but not before God.

Romans 3:21-4:2

By reading the complete text in the third and fourth chapters of Romans, we see some of the world changing discoveries that Abraham made. I, strongly, recommend that after reading this chapter, you read those two chapters in Romans and meditate on these before moving on.

Let me list some here for you to make it easier.

The righteousness of God by Christ is unto all that believe.....there is no difference

So there is nobody on the face of the earth, no man of God that has access to God more than I do. Elijah was a prominent prophet who thought he was the only one left and God had to remind him that there were seven thousand other prophets. I believe there are thousands of non-prominent prophets that God has placed around you. People who are recognised in Heaven. By the grace of God, I am one that Heaven recognises.

As soon as you start esteeming other people higher than yourself, you start to run into challenges. People start to take the place of God in your life and the sin of idolatry silently slips in. The words of others become greater than the personal discoveries you have made leading you to devalue one of the greatest assets you have as a believer.

Justification comes freely by grace.....for the remission of sins

There is no monetary value you can place on the things of God. As soon as money is made a pre-requisite for the things of God, we create a challenge for the people. Is God only the God of the rich? There is nothing we have discussed here that requires you have any money. Irrespective of your financial status, you have the time to make these discoveries. Giving is important and the gospel cannot be complete if the teaching on giving is taken out of it. After all, God started this faith journey by giving His Son but giving money as a direct exchange for the Holy Ghost is a sure path to heartache.

A man is justified by faith without the deeds of the law

This is an extremely powerful truth. Firstly, fulfilling the Law of Moses if you were not a Jew or born into the family of Israel would be an almost impossible task. Even those to whom the law was given struggled to keep it. Besides, there were issues with the law. It was not all God. Some of it was given by Moses because of the hardness of the hearts of the people.

For example, there were instructions on marriage that deviated from the original plan of God. Furthermore, having to go to Jerusalem to worship would immediately have made fulfilling the law something that only the rich could contemplate. The Eunuch that we read about in *Acts 8:27* was obviously a man of means given his position relative to the Queen of Ethiopia. Thankfully, without all these deeds of the law, we would still get a seal of approval from God if we believe. How awesome!

Secondly, there are laws that have been put in place governing the affairs of life. This means that if you legitimately find yourself in a difficult place, applying these principles we are talking about will supersede even the laws of nature to ensure that your need is met.

In the story of Jesus and the fig tree in *Mark 4*, Jesus expected the tree to respond to him even though the external seasons of life dictated something else. Both Sarah and Abraham were past the age of child bearing yet their bodies responded to faith. Joshua was in a war and required nature to support him and it did. I hope you understand the picture now. There may be laws governing the things you are believing for but the most important thing is for you to connect with the unseen because once you have done that, the unseen will surely come to pass irrespective of the limitations that naturral laws may dictate. This is why the statement from Jesus that says, "*...all things are possible to him that believeth*" suddenly makes a lot of sense.

Faith did not invalidate the law. Faith established the law

I mention time and time again that "*there is nothing in the New Testament that the Old Testament did not foretell.*" The prophecy of the *new creation* (*2 Corinthians 5:17*) was in the Old Testament. The revelation of tongues was also there not to mention the numerous prophetic landmarks that talked about the experiences Jesus was going to have. There is almost no miracle Jesus performed in the New Testament that you will not find an equivalent in the Old Testament. For example, Jesus fed four thousand people on one occasion and five thousand on another but Elisha also did something similar when the one hundred people were fed with twenty loaves. Jesus raised the dead but we also have accounts of people who had their dead raised in the Old Testament. Jesus turned water to wine in the Cana but both Elijah and Elisha did miracles that were not too different from this. Even casting out of devils was something that was a common practice before the time of Jesus otherwise Jesus, in *Matthew 12:27*, would not have asked the question, *"...If I by Beelzebub cast out devils, by who, do your children cast them out?..."* Jesus' disciples, in *Mark 9:38*, would also not have found someone *"casting out devils in thy name."*

While we no longer need to go to Jerusalem to worship God, we still need to worship God. Faith makes the practice of serving God more accessible to people. Don't be deceived, with the exception of a few cases, what was a sin under the law is still a sin under grace. While I was thinking on this, a thought dropped in my heart saying, *"there is nothing in my future that my past has not hinted me about."* A lot of people have been ignoring these hints and prompts because they have not connected with picture of the unseen.

The seal of the righteousness of faith is received while being uncircumcised

There is nothing you will receive from God that you will receive on the basis of it being your right because of something you have done. Abraham received this seal of righteous while he was uncircumcised and those that were with him were uncircumcised so it was not the circumcision that qualified him for faith.

So the revelation that takes you from unbelief to faith

was not one that came when you were in faith. Even in your unbelief, God is gracious enough to have mercy on you. How much more loving do we want Him to be? The Scriptures tell us that while we were yet sinners, Christ died for us. Even if we are unfaithful, God remains faithful.

The key point with these discoveries that Abraham made is that there is no basis for anyone anywhere to accept any physical limitation as an insurmountable hurdle in life. These five discoveries, amongst others, are some of the cornerstones on which faith operates.

Chapter 6
OVERCOMING TRADITION

F aith is one of the fundamental building blocks any Christian needs to please God. In *Hebrews 11:6*, the Bible says, *"but without faith it is impossible to please Him..."* There are so many examples in the New Testament that depict faith as being the critical ingredient in contacting the supernatural for natural results. We have the woman with the issue of blood in *Mark 5:25* to whom Jesus said, *"Daughter, thy faith hath made thee whole..."*, the Centurion in *Matthew 8:10* and the Canaanite woman in *Matthew 15:28* both of whom got commended for their great faith.

Let us also not forget the story of the crippled man in *Acts 14: 8-10* that *"...had faith to be healed..."* and the numerous other stories of deliverance, sustenance and provision that were all based on faith recorded in the Bible. Despite these examples in Scriptures, why does *"faith"* appear to be that elusive to most people in this generation? Why do those that profess God appear to be more like beggars than princes? Why is there a wide gap between what we claim we believe and the tangible results we have to show?

With God having set faith as a necessary requirement for pleasing Him, would He not make it relatively easy to acquire it? Is God trying to make Himself difficult to find or have we just misunderstood the process for acquiring faith? These are some of the questions that led me to check some of the most common Scriptures about faith with a view of discovering what we may have missed or what may have been communicated to us inaccurately by tradition.

This *"tradition"* the Merriam-Webster dictionary describes as an *"inherited, established, or customary pattern of thought, action or behaviour (as a religious practice or a social custom)."* This is very crucial because thought patterns imbibed as a religious practice are not easily transformed and need consistent application of the Word of God. I'm sure someone would ask why?

Firstly, you may need to deal with reputational impact. Remember the story of Herod and John the Baptist. Even though Herod had very high regard for John, He still ordered his execution.

> [20] *For Herod feared John, knowing that he was a just man and an holy, and observed him; and when he heard him, he did many things, and heard him gladly.*
> [26] *And the king was exceeding sorry; yet for his oath's sake, and for their sakes which sat with him, he would not reject her.*
> [27] *And immediately the king sent an executioner, and commanded his head to be brought: and he went and beheaded him in the prison,*
>
> Mark 6:20,26

Secondly, the cost of starting with the new thought pattern may be considered too high. Remember the story of the rich man who asked Jesus what to do to have eternal life and to whom Jesus told to keep the ten-commandments of Moses.

> [20] *The young man saith unto him, All these things have I kept from my youth up: what lack I yet?*
> [21] *Jesus said unto him, If thou wilt be perfect, go and sell that thou hast, and give to the poor, and thou shalt have treasure in heaven:*

and come and follow me.
²² But when the young man heard that saying, he went away sorrowful: for he had great possessions.

Matthew 19:20-22

Thirdly, there may be an impact on the financial status or a threat to the livelihood of the person. When financial losses are involved, people can behave in very erratic ways.

¹⁶ And it came to pass, as we went to prayer, a certain damsel possessed with a spirit of divination met us, which brought her masters much gain by soothsaying:
¹⁷ The same followed Paul and us, and cried, saying, These men are the servants of the most high God, which shew unto us the way of salvation.
¹⁸ And this did she many days. But Paul, being grieved, turned and said to the spirit, I command thee in the name of Jesus Christ to come out of her. And he came out the same hour.
¹⁹ And when her masters saw that the hope of their gains was gone, they caught Paul and Silas, and drew them into the marketplace unto the rulers,
²⁰ And brought them to the magistrates, saying, These men, being Jews, do exceedingly trouble our city,
²¹ And teach customs, which are not lawful for us to receive, neither to observe, being Romans.

Acts 16:16-21

So whatever the reason for holding a particular thought or behaviour, traditions make the Word of God ineffective.

In *Mark 7:5-13*, Jesus' response to the Pharisees and Scribes vividly paints the picture of how tradition makes the Word of God ineffective.

⁵ Then the Pharisees and scribes asked him, Why walk not thy disciples according to the tradition of the elders, but eat bread with

~ 55 ~

unwashen hands?

⁶ He answered and said unto them, Well hath Esaias prophesied of you hypocrites, as it is written, This people honoureth me with their lips, but their heart is far from me.

⁷ Howbeit in vain do they worship me, teaching for doctrines the commandments of men.

⁸ For laying aside the commandment of God, ye hold the tradition of men, as the washing of pots and cups: and many other such like things ye do.

⁹ And he said unto them, Full well ye reject the commandment of God, that ye may keep your own tradition. ¹⁰ For Moses said, Honour thy father and thy mother; and, Whoso curseth father or mother, let him die the death:

¹¹ But ye say, If a man shall say to his father or mother, It is Corban, that is to say, a gift, by whatsoever thou mightest be profited by me; he shall be free.

¹² And ye suffer him no more to do ought for his father or his mother;

¹³ Making the word of God of none effect through your tradition, which ye have delivered: and many such like things do ye

Mark 7:5-13

Through their actions, the Pharisees and the Scribes were making it impossible for the power of the Word of God to produce an effect in their lives. In this present day, these people would have been in Church. The Pharisees religiously accepted the written Word of God as inspired by God but insisted that traditions had equal authority. Though they were a minority in the Jewish Ruling Council, they were powerful and had the support of the common man. The masses are one of the biggest hindrances to a change in tradition. The people do not have to be supportive for it to be God. Most things of God are initially rejected by the people. Jesus came to His own and His own received Him not.

What Paul had to say about tradition

> *6 As ye have therefore received Christ Jesus the Lord, so walk ye in him:*
> *7 Rooted and built up in him, and stablished in the faith, as ye have been taught, abounding therein with thanksgiving.*
> *8 Beware lest any man spoil you through philosophy and vain deceit, after the tradition of men, after the rudiments of the world, and not after Christ.*
> *9 For in him dwelleth all the fulness of the Godhead bodily.*
> *10 And ye are complete in him, which is the head of all principality and power:*
>
> *Colossians 2:6-10.*

Am I held by tradition?

Being bound by tradition is a very dangerous place to be because everything looks like God. You have all the trappings of religion but the God you purport to serve is not a guest at the party. Let us look at three areas you could check to confirm where you stand.

1. *The result of the Word of God is not apparent in your life.*

   If most things in your life can be easily achieved without God, then you may have a problem. Is the finger of God apparent? Are the red sea's in your life parting, is the Jordan opening up so you can pass on dry land? Are you succeeding where others are failing?

   According to *James 2:17-18,* Faith needs to be shown by works and not just words. If the words are coming out and the works are not, we need to check the source of the words. It may be that the lips are honouring God but the heart is far.

When John sent people to Jesus to ask if He was the Christ, He immediately healed some people and told John's disciples to go back and tell John what they had seen (*Matthew 11:2-5*).

2. *You believe the Word of God but...*

Like the Pharisee's, you hold a supporting view to the Word of God. Scriptures are interpreted in a way that changes what the Word of God actually says. The text we looked at in *Mark 7:5-13* already explains this.

3. *Handling the Word of God like a constitution*

You are treating the Word of God like a constitution that needs a 2nd or 3rd amendment and requires the ratification of a council. We think Scriptures are in need of modernisation and we want to get on with the times. In *Hebrews 4:3*, we see that the gospel has been consistent over time. It is the "same gospel" that was preached to us that was preached to them. I always say that the accuracy of prophecy does not increase with spiritual maturity. If you are truly moved by the Holy Ghost, you will be accurate 100% of the time. What improves is your ability to hear God. You learn to suppress the voice of the flesh.

I do agree that revelation is progressive but the new does not invalidate the old. The new fulfils the old. The Old Testament told us to expect the New Testament and there is nothing in the New Testament that the Old Testament did not foretell.

How do I get out of tradition?

This story highlights the importance of not just going to a Church or a religious gathering to take in everything that is said. You need to build a culture of verifying things in scriptures. In *Luke 2:46,* Jesus was in the temple sitting in the midst of the "doctors" not "doctor" of the law. He was in the temple with an inquisitive mind. He not only listened to the doctors but also asked them questions. A person who does not ask questions will remain ignorant and faithless. You cannot operate in faith effectively with unanswered questions because unanswered questions feed doubt. Answered questions strengthen your faith even when the physical evidence has not yet manifested.

The God behind the Scriptures is always eager to answer questions from a genuine heart. While God speaks through His servants, He is also keen on speaking to us as individuals. What you discover from Scriptures yourself is usually more powerful than what is communicated to you by others. What is communicated to you by others should lead you to a verification process. Omitting this verification process is actually risky as you may be assimilating facts that were incorrectly presented even though the speaker had good intentions.

> [10] And the brethren immediately sent away Paul and Silas by night unto Berea: who coming thither went into the synagogue of the Jews.
> [11] These were more noble than those in Thessalonica, in that they received the word with all readiness of mind, and searched the scriptures daily, whether those things were so.
>
> *Acts 17:10-11*

The Amplified Bible even gives us more insight into what happened in Berea concerning the message that was preached and we will discuss this "message" later.

10 Now the brethren at once sent Paul and Silas away by night to Beroea; and when they arrived, they entered the synagogue of the Jews.
11 Now these [Jews] were better disposed and more noble than those in Thessalonica, for they were entirely ready and accepted and welcomed the message [concerning the attainment through Christ of eternal salvation in the kingdom of God] with inclination of mind and eagerness, searching and examining the Scriptures daily to see if these things were so.

Acts 17:10-11 (AMP)

Chapter 7
TURNING FAITH LOOSE

In previous chapters, we have talked about faith, we have touched on how to build and nourish that faith to keep it active. We have talked about the importance of faith. We all know that you cannot talk about the message of Christianity without talking about faith. I don't need to remind you of the popular phrase from *Mark 9:23* that says, *"...All things are possible to him that believeth..."*

For a lot of people, that statement reads more like, *"... All things are possible to him that believeth...except paying my bills, getting healed in my body, bringing solutions to my community or making a difference in life..."* For them, the statement then just becomes something like an extra tyre in a car. It never gets used unless you have a flat. We use faith like a fire extinguisher - it stays inactive until there is a fire getting out of control.

Growing up in Nigeria many years ago, in one of the houses we lived in, we used to have a water-tank at the back of the house so anytime the mains went dry, we had water for a while. It was a reservoir of sustenance. When some people realized that there was a water-tank, sometimes, they would try to get water from the tank so we had to put padlocks on the tap to prevent unauthorized access. The challenge for a lot of modern day Christians, is that faith is still in locked up in a reservoir. The challenges of life are not overcome by those who have a reservoir, they are overcome by those who use what is in the reservoir.

The travesty of life is that many people will go through life without having used the contents of their reservoir. More worrying, others will use the experiences of these ones who failed to justify why things are the way they are in their own lives. For many people for whom things have not worked out well, there are many, under the same circumstances, it worked for. Though many make losses during a recession, others also make incredible profits in the same period. Many are starved of ideas and complain about what the economy and those running things have done to them yet in the same atmosphere some big business have been started. For example;

Microsoft was started during the 1973-1975 recession. At present, its annual revenue is over US$60b. When asked in a recent interview, its founder said a lot of his charity work in inspired by religious morality. In order words, Christian ethics have a strong influence on what he does for humanity.

FedEx was incorporated in 1971 as Federal Express, but didn't begin operations until the 1973 recession. Federal Express was born from a Yale term paper written by Frederick Smith. It is claimed his professor said he would only get a C if the idea was feasible. He *started* with 14 aircraft, deliveries to 25 cities and 389 employees.

Smith was crippled by bone disease as a small boy but regained his health by age 10, before becoming an excellent football player and learning to fly at 15. He went to a Presbyterian School. Presently, FedEx has 628 aircraft, over 90,000 delivery vehicles and more than 300,000 employees resulting in US$40b in annual revenue.

General Electric was founded in the depression of 1873 by inventor Thomas Edison, creator of the incandescent light bulb. The depression saw half of the nation's railroads declare bankruptcy and half of the country's iron furnaces shut down. What was started by a single investment bank shutting down led to what is now called a panic, but Edison opened a small laboratory in 1876 that would later become General Electric. Today, GE has more than 300,000 employees and a cash hoard of more than US$88 billion.

One of the greatest moments to start something great is when the external pressures and contrary forces appear the strongest. The individual religious persuasions of these people is not what is important here. It is the fact you cannot use the limitations of the environment to justify failure. Failure is not caused by the strength of the contrary force but by your internal persuasion to give-up on a pursuit. I think, for the purpose of this message, it is better for us to consider the personal religious persuasions of the people I have just mentioned as non-Christian. At least, that way, you will have a context of what is power within you is capable of. Of course, it is crucial, that we do not use the external to judge the limitations of what is within. What you see was created by the unseen therefore it is impossible for the created to be greater that the creator.

It is therefore important for us to understand how to use what is in the reservoir profitably.

Let us look at Hebrews 4:1-2

> [1] *Let us therefore fear, lest, a promise being left us of entering into*

his rest, any of you should seem to come short of it.
² For unto us was the gospel preached, as well as unto them: but the word (gospel) preached did not profit them, not being mixed with faith in them that heard it.

² For indeed we have had the glad tidings [Gospel of God] proclaimed to us just as truly as they [the Israelites of old did when the good news of deliverance from bondage came to them]; but the message they heard did not benefit them, because it was not mixed with faith (with [c]the leaning of the entire personality on God in absolute trust and confidence in His power, wisdom, and goodness) by those who heard it; [d]neither were they united in faith with the ones [Joshua and Caleb] who heard (did believe).

Hebrews 4:2 (AMP)

Before I get into the crux of the message on how to turn your faith loose, there are three key words in this verse that we need to understand in order. Gospel, Profit, Faith. I say in order because for the mathematically inclined, you will notice that the writer is trying to describe a formula. The literal translation in the order presented by the writer is:

$$\text{Gospel} - \text{Mixing Process} + \text{Faith} \neq \text{Profit}$$

Putting this in the order in which we have been trained we would get:

$$\text{Gospel} + \text{Faith} + \textit{Mixing Process} = \text{Profit}$$

For ease of understanding, I will take "faith" before I take "profit and leave mixing process for today.

The Gospel
In the Old Testament, the word "gospel" referred to the good news of God's kindness, particularly the Messianic blessings. The Messianic blessings are the blessings that

were linked to the coming of a Messiah. These are mainly the Scriptures that are an allegory for Christ. When you browse through them, if someone does not tell you, you may not realize that they are talking about Jesus. There are many Scriptures in the Old Testament that if you take the message of Christ out, they make no sense, particularly, in the book of Isaiah.

For example,

> *[14]Therefore the Lord himself shall give you a sign; Behold, a virgin shall conceive, and bear a son, and shall call his name Immanuel.*
>
> *Isaiah 7:14*

> *[7] He was oppressed, and he was afflicted, yet he opened not his mouth: he is brought as a lamb to the slaughter, and as a sheep before her shearers is dumb, so he openeth not his mouth.*
> *[8] He was taken from prison and from judgment: and who shall declare his generation? for he was cut off out of the land of the living: for the transgression of my people was he stricken.*
> *[9] And he made his grave with the wicked, and with the rich in his death; because he had done no violence, neither was any deceit in his mouth.*
> *[10] Yet it pleased the LORD to bruise him; he hath put him to grief: when thou shalt make his soul an offering for sin, he shall see his seed, he shall prolong his days, and the pleasure of the LORD shall prosper in his hand.*
> *[11] He shall see of the travail of his soul, and shall be satisfied: by his knowledge shall my righteous servant justify many; for he shall bear their iniquities.*
> *[12] Therefore will I divide him a portion with the great, and he shall divide the spoil with the strong; because he hath poured out his soul unto death: and he was numbered with the transgressors; and he bare the sin of many, and made intercession for the transgressors.*
>
> *Isaiah 53:7-12*

When reading Scriptures, there are a number of categories you can put them in. Some of which include:

1. *Historical Accounts:*

   These are just stories of things that happened in the past. For example, the parting of the Red Sea, the plagues of Egypt, The walls of Jericho, Elijah and the prophets of Baal. Elisha's bones raising a dead body. These give you an idea of what God is capable of doing with people, to people and for people.

2. *Active Accounts:*

   These, like the first category, are things that happened and as a result of them happening, certain courses of action are open to us today. An example of this would be Jesus healing the sick that the prophetic words in Scriptures may be fulfill. *Matthew 8:16-17* tells of how Jesus healed many people that were possessed with devils and healed all that were sick *that it might be fulfilled that which was spoken by Isaiah the prophet,* saying, Himself took our infirmities and bare our sicknesses. He bore them once and for all and there is no record of Him giving the sicknesses back. These are really just like a contractual clause in a contract. We invoke them if the need arises. This is not something God is going to do. We have already been healed by the stripes of Jesus. If sickness wants to take hold, we invoke the contractual clause on health and healing. If its poverty, then invoke the relevant clause that applies. He became poor that I might be rich.

3. *Promissory Notes:*

   These are things that God in Christ has promised

us. These are things that are going to happen in due course and the fulfilment of which depends on whether the individual wants them or not. For example, the promise of the infilling of the Spirit. In *Acts 2:38-39*. Peter described the infilling as a promise available. *John 16:7...but if I depart, I will send him to you..."* *John 16:23-24*. Whatsoever you shall ask the father in my name, He will give it to you...Hitherto, you have asked nothing in my name ask and you shall receive that your joy may be full.

Why is this distinction important? If all you hear is historical accounts, you will get offended with God and will not have the confidence to re-create historical accounts.

In *Judges 6:13*, Gideon sounded an angry man when the angel appeared to him.

> [11] *And there came an angel of the Lord, and sat under an oak which was in Ophrah, that pertained unto Joash the Abiezrite: and his son Gideon threshed wheat by the winepress, to hide it from the Midianites.*
> [12] *And the angel of the Lord appeared unto him, and said unto him, The Lord is with thee, thou mighty man of valour.*
> [13] *And Gideon said unto him, Oh my Lord, if the LORD be with us, why then is all this befallen us? and where be all his miracles which our fathers told us of, saying, Did not the LORD bring us up from Egypt? but now the LORD hath forsaken us, and delivered us into the hands of the Midianites.*

Judges 6:13

Active Accounts and Promissory Notes allow you to re-create historical accounts. Within what I call Active Accounts and Promissory Notes, it is very important for us to look for the Scriptures that paint a picture of a living

Jesus. Even the Holy Spirit, has a major assignment (*John 15:26*) – He shall testify of Me.

In *John 5:39-40*, in the Amplified Bible, Jesus said, *"You search and investigate and pore over the Scriptures diligently, because you suppose and trust that you have eternal life through them. And these [very Scriptures] testify about Me! 40 And still you are not willing [but refuse] to come to Me, so that you might have life."* Sometimes we get so engrossed in the things of God and have no time for God.

In *Acts 8:26-35*, The Ethopian Eunuch struggled with the writing of Isaiah until Philip came and explained Christ to Him.

> ²⁶ *And the angel of the Lord spake unto Philip, saying, Arise, and go toward the south unto the way that goeth down from Jerusalem unto Gaza, which is desert.*
> ²⁷ *And he arose and went: and, behold, a man of Ethiopia, an eunuch of great authority under Candace queen of the Ethiopians, who had the charge of all her treasure, and had come to Jerusalem for to worship,*
> ²⁸ *Was returning, and sitting in his chariot read Esaias the prophet.*
> ²⁹ *Then the Spirit said unto Philip, Go near, and join thyself to this chariot.*
> ³⁰ *And Philip ran thither to him, and heard him read the prophet Esaias, and said, Understandest thou what thou readest?*
> ³¹ *And he said, How can I, except some man should guide me? And he desired Philip that he would come up and sit with him.*
> ³² *The place of the scripture which he read was this, He was led as a sheep to the slaughter; and like a lamb dumb before his shearer, so opened he not his mouth:*
> ³³ *In his humiliation his judgment was taken away: and who shall declare his generation? for his life is taken from the earth.*
> ³⁴ *And the eunuch answered Philip, and said, I pray thee, of whom speaketh the prophet this? of himself, or of some other man?*
> ³⁵ *Then Philip opened his mouth, and began at the same scripture, and preached unto him Jesus.*

³⁶ And as they went on their way, they came unto a certain water: and the eunuch said, See, here is water; what doth hinder me to be baptized?
³⁷ And Philip said, If thou believest with all thine heart, thou mayest. And he answered and said, I believe that Jesus Christ is the Son of God.

Acts 8:26-35

The writer of the book of Romans, in *Romans 10:15-16* also highlighted something important. The gospel was also preached to them.

¹⁵ And how shall they preach, except they be sent? as it is written, How beautiful are the feet of them that preach the gospel of peace, and bring glad tidings of good things!
¹⁶ But they have not all obeyed the gospel. For Esaias saith, Lord, who hath believed our report?
¹⁷ So then faith cometh by hearing, and hearing by the word of God.

Romans 10:15-16.

The New Testament's use of the word "gospel" is not really different. It is about the glad tidings of the coming kingdom of God. The main difference now is that the Kingdom (*the dominion and authority of God*) is within you. So the gospel is not just the message that Jesus died on the Cross for a cause. Many have died and still die for causes they believe in. It is not just the fact that Jesus was raised on the 3rd day. There are stories of people who were dead longer than the time Jesus was dead. In *John 11:39* it is stated about Lazarus, "*...for he hath been dead four days.*" There are many who had been certified dead and have been raised from the dead by believers. Some of you here will also raise people from the dead if Jesus tarries. Bodies that have been dead for days will be raised. Some people are dead today because we have taken death as the ultimate sentence. If Jesus had not intervened, Lazarus would have remained dead. If Paul did not intervene

Eutychus would have died. If Elisha did not intervene, the Shunnammite woman's son would have died. If you do not intervene, some people would remain dead.

The power of the message of Christ is in the fact that He was raised from the dead and remains alive. This means, death, the greatest enemy has no more power over Him and because He is alive, he can impart humanity with divinity. He said;

> [18] *I am he that liveth, and was dead; and, behold, I am alive for evermore, Amen; and have the keys of hell and of death.*
>
> *Revelation 1:18*

> [14] *For it is evident that our Lord sprang out of Juda; of which tribe Moses spake nothing concerning priesthood.*
> [15] *And it is yet far more evident: for that after the similitude of Melchisedec there ariseth another priest,*
> [16] *Who is made, not after the law of a carnal commandment, but after the power of an endless life.*
> [17] *For he testifieth, Thou art a priest for ever after the order of Melchisedec.*
>
> *Hebrews 7:14-17*

So when you want to turn your faith loose, there is an understanding of the word "gospel" that is important. We are talking about a living Jesus that is right here with us. Not a Jesus that deserted us and ran away to Heaven and leaving us to fight the earthly battle ourselves. It is the understanding you get from someone sent to you by God regarding the Scriptures that were already burning in your heart. When you hear the message, immediately, light will come and you will see what you need to do to break into the next level.

Faith

> [2] *For unto us was the gospel preached, as well as unto them: but the word (gospel) preached did not profit them, not being mixed with faith in them that heard it.*

Let us not forget the formula we are dissecting.

Gospel + Faith + Mixing Process = Profit

The writer of Hebrews is saying that when you add faith to the gospel, you should make gains. We will talk about this gains in a moment but notice the three parts. So we have the gospel and faith passed through a mixing process to create gains. Faith is a raw material, very distinct from the gospel that goes into the mixing process. I hope you have noticed that the mixing process is not faith. In *Matthew 6:6-8*, Jesus told his disciples to beware of people who think God will hear them because of the process – vain repetitions.

> [6] *But thou, when thou prayest, enter into thy closet, and when thou hast shut thy door, pray to thy Father which is in secret; and thy Father which seeth in secret shall reward thee openly.*
> [7] *But when ye pray, use not vain repetitions, as the heathen do: for they think that they shall be heard for their much speaking.*
> [8] *Be not ye therefore like unto them: for your Father knoweth what things ye have need of, before ye ask him.*

> *Matthew 6:6-8*

Faith in this context, refers to your capacity, while in prayer, to visualize a definite outcome made possible through the limitless power of the Word of God.

In *Mark 9:14-29*, Jesus came in contact with a man whose son was possessed with a dumb and deaf Spirit. In *verse 22*, the man says something,

14 And when he came to his disciples, he saw a great multitude about them, and the scribes questioning with them.

15 And straightway all the people, when they beheld him, were greatly amazed, and running to him saluted him.

16 And he asked the scribes, What question ye with them?

17 And one of the multitude answered and said, Master, I have brought unto thee my son, which hath a dumb spirit;

18 And wheresoever he taketh him, he teareth him: and he foameth, and gnasheth with his teeth, and pineth away: and I spake to thy disciples that they should cast him out; and they could not.

19 He answereth him, and saith, O faithless generation, how long shall I be with you? how long shall I suffer you? bring him unto me.

20 And they brought him unto him: and when he saw him, straightway the spirit tare him; and he fell on the ground, and wallowed foaming.

21 And he asked his father, How long is it ago since this came unto him? And he said, Of a child.

22 And ofttimes it hath cast him into the fire, and into the waters, to destroy him: but if thou canst do any thing, have compassion on us, and help us.

23 Jesus said unto him, If thou canst believe, all things are possible to him that believeth.

24 And straightway the father of the child cried out, and said with tears, Lord, I believe; help thou mine unbelief.

25 When Jesus saw that the people came running together, he rebuked the foul spirit, saying unto him, Thou dumb and deaf spirit, I charge thee, come out of him, and enter no more into him.

26 And the spirit cried, and rent him sore, and came out of him: and he was as one dead; insomuch that many said, He is dead.

27 But Jesus took him by the hand, and lifted him up; and he arose.

28 And when he was come into the house, his disciples asked him privately, Why could not we cast him out?

29 And he said unto them, This kind can come forth by nothing, but by prayer and fasting.

Mark 9:14-29

The word *"help"* in *verse 24* there literally means *"give me the view, intelligence or understanding of a wise-man that is able to change of perspective."* Notice that this man had already gone to the Disciples who had tried and it did not succeed. Jesus' response to their question of why they could not cast out the devil was simple. Some challenges require prayer and fasting. The account in *Matthew 17* gives a slightly different perspective. *Matthew 17:20* shows that Jesus addressed unbelief before addressing prayer and fasting.

Look at the numerous miracles of Jesus where he touched on faith. Almost all of them had to do with the people visualizing what was possible with their encounter with Jesus ever before they got to him:

> In *Matthew 9:21*, in the story of the woman with the issue of blood, it is recorded that "*...she said within herself, if I may but touch his garment, I shall be whole...*" This was something she said before getting to Jesus. This position must have been informed by some information she had.
>
> In *Matthew 8*, in the story of a centurion whose servant was sick of the palsy, the centurion answered and said, "*Lord, I am not worthy that thou shouldest come under my roof: but speak the word only, and my servant shall be healed. For I am a man under authority, having soldiers under me: and I say to this man, Go, and he goeth; and to another, Come, and he cometh; and to my servant, Do this, and he doeth it.*" Again, in this story, the Centurion had compared the authority he had in his position over other soldiers to the authority Jesus had over sickness.

Let us add one from the Old Testament for completeness.

In *2 Kings 4*, In the story of the Shunnammite woman, we see this same concept of visualisation at work again,

20 And when he had taken him, and brought him to his mother, he sat on her knees till noon, and then died.
21 And she went up, and laid him on the bed of the man of God, and shut the door upon him, and went out.
22 And she called unto her husband, and said, Send me, I pray thee, one of the young men, and one of the asses, that I may run to the man of God, and come again.

2 Kings 4:20-22

Profit

2 For unto us was the gospel preached, as well as unto them: but the word (gospel) preached did not profit them, not being mixed with faith in them that heard it.

The impact of combining the gospel with faith is profit. I like the way the Merriam-Webster dictionary defines profit. It called it *valuable return*. The VisualThesaurus, among its many definitions, calls it, *the advantageous quality of being beneficial*. It means after all activities put together, you have more than you started with. So for this people, there was no profit. The energy they expended in the pursuit of the things of God was greater than the results they achieved. If the results on the outside are not far exceeding the effort you contributed, your faith may be dormant. The workings of God should far exceed your request and your thoughts. He is able to do exceedingly abundantly above *all* we ask or think according to the power that is at work within us.

The degree to which your thoughts and requests are exceeded is a reflection of how wide your reservoir is opened. Let us not deceive ourselves, In the parable of the sower, in *Mark 4:20*, do you notice that Jesus did not actually paint the picture of different seed. Every seed had the potential to produce results. It was the environment that determined what happened to the seed not the sower.

> ²⁰ And these are they which are sown on good ground; such as hear the word, and receive it, and bring forth fruit, some thirtyfold, some sixty, and some an hundred.

So the minimum payback you should be looking for is 30%.

> ²⁶ And he said, So is the kingdom of God, as if a man should cast seed into the ground;
> ²⁷ And should sleep, and rise night and day, and the seed should spring and grow up, he knoweth not how.
> ²⁸ For the earth bringeth forth fruit of herself; first the blade, then the ear, after that the full corn in the ear.
> ²⁹ But when the fruit is brought forth, immediately he putteth in the sickle, because the harvest is come.
> ³⁰ And he said, Whereunto shall we liken the kingdom of God? or with what comparison shall we compare it?
> ³¹ It is like a grain of mustard seed, which, when it is sown in the earth, is less than all the seeds that be in the earth:
> ³² But when it is sown, it groweth up, and becometh greater than all herbs, and shooteth out great branches; so that the fowls of the air may lodge under the shadow of it.
> ³³ And with many such parables spake he the word unto them, as they were able to hear it.
> ³⁴ But without a parable spake he not unto them: and when they were alone, he expounded all things to his disciples.

> *Mark 4:26-34.*

How do I turn my Faith loose?

So how do I turn my faith loose? How do I get what is in the reservoir to come out? Let me give you five quick pointers.

1. *Reach out for something greater than you*

    Faith is not faith until there is something greater than you to reach out to. If you do not have a vision, you cannot have active faith so get a vision. I believe there is no one making giant strides in life that did not define a future state when they were in a state when their desired future state looked unattainable. You need to build hope in that future state and wait for salvation with joy and full confidence that the possibility of achieving the desired future state is possible. And there is no restriction on what that future state could be.

2. *Understand that potential is unlimited but current capacity is limited*

    In the Parable of the Talent in *Matthew 25:15*. Talents were distributed *severally according to their ability*. Jesus did not overload the disciples. In *John 16:12-13*, He said, "*... I have many things to say unto you but you cannot bear them now...*" When capacity stretches significantly beyond vision, waste is inevitable. In John 6:12, Jesus said, "*...Gather up the fragments that remain, that nothing be lost.*"

3. *Your preparation demonstrates your expectation. Start making preparation for the next level.*

    Mary went to meet Elizabeth for a sign that would strengthen her faith. Jesus told his disciples, "*... make the men sit down...*" No preparation means no faith. Every woman expecting a baby makes preparation for the delivery of the child. If you believe, start making preparations for the next level.

4. Do not look for short-cuts

Jesus could have asked for Angels but the purpose was greater. It was a deliberate choice not to use his power. My general advise here is, particularly in relation to financial issues, do not look for debt cancellation. Look for the capacity to pay. Do not confuse access to credit to wealth creation. That you have good credit rating is not synonymous with wealth creation.. Your reward is not based on your potential but on your current capacity to produce.

5. Prophetic assistance

God honours the words of his servants particularly, those He has placed as gifts in the body to function in the five-fold ministries. Sometimes, physical actions, in response to prophetic commands should be obeyed for the completion of your faith. Some of these actions may not really look like they make sense but that notwithstanding, obey and you will prosper.

[19] *And the men of the city said unto Elisha, Behold, I pray thee, the situation of this city is pleasant, as my lord seeth: but the water is naught, and the ground barren.*

[20] *And he said, Bring me a new cruse, and put salt therein. And they brought it to him.*

[21] *And he went forth unto the spring of the waters, and cast the salt in there, and said, Thus saith the Lord, I have healed these waters; there shall not be from thence any more death or barren land.*

[22] *So the waters were healed unto this day, according to the saying of Elisha which he spake.*

2 Kings 2:19-22

⁸ And it was so, when Elisha the man of God had heard that the king of Israel had rent his clothes, that he sent to the king, saying, Wherefore hast thou rent thy clothes? let him come now to me, and he shall know that there is a prophet in Israel.

⁹ So Naaman came with his horses and with his chariot, and stood at the door of the house of Elisha.

¹⁰ And Elisha sent a messenger unto him, saying, Go and wash in Jordan seven times, and thy flesh shall come again to thee, and thou shalt be clean.

¹¹ But Naaman was wroth, and went away, and said, Behold, I thought, He will surely come out to me, and stand, and call on the name of the Lord his God, and strike his hand over the place, and recover the leper.

¹² Are not Abana and Pharpar, rivers of Damascus, better than all the waters of Israel? may I not wash in them, and be clean? So he turned and went away in a rage.

¹³ And his servants came near, and spake unto him, and said, My father, if the prophet had bid thee do some great thing, wouldest thou not have done it? how much rather then, when he saith to thee, Wash, and be clean?

¹⁴ Then went he down, and dipped himself seven times in Jordan, according to the saying of the man of God: and his flesh came again like unto the flesh of a little child, and he was clean.

2 Kings 5:8-15

Chapter 8
OUTPOURING OF THE SPIRIT

As the Body of Christ, particularly a local assembly, enters a season of the Outpouring of the Spirit, it is important for God's people to see what the Word of God has to say about operations and manifestations of the Spirit as described in *1 Corinthians 12: 1-11.* A move of the Spirit that is not understood by the Church can be, very easily, lost.

In *Ephesians 4:30,* Paul, the Apostle, warns the Church not to *"...grieve the Holy Spirit of God, whereby ye are sealed unto the day of redemption."* He further emphasizes, in his writing to the Corinthian Church, his desire to ensure that Believer's were not misinformed concerning operations and manifestations of the Holy Spirit.

> *¹ Now concerning spiritual gifts, brethren, I would not have you ignorant.*
>
> 1 Corinthians 12:1

> *¹ Now about the spiritual gifts (the special endowments of supernatural energy), brethren, I do not want you to be misinformed.*
>
> 1 Corinthians 12:1 (AMP)

To fully understand what the Apostle was talking about, let us look at how he describes these operations and manifestations of the Spirit.

> *¹ Now about the spiritual gifts (the special endowments of supernatural energy), brethren, I do not want you to be misinformed.*

² *You know that when you were heathen, you were led off after idols that could not speak [habitually] as impulse directed and whenever the occasion might arise.*

³ *Therefore I want you to understand that no one speaking under the power and influence of the [Holy] Spirit of God can [ever] say, Jesus be cursed! And no one can [really] say, Jesus is [my] Lord, except by and under the power and influence of the Holy Spirit.*

⁴ *Now there are distinctive varieties and distributions of endowments (gifts, extraordinary powers distinguishing certain Christians, due to the power of divine grace operating in their souls by the Holy Spirit) and they vary, but the [Holy] Spirit remains the same.*

⁵ *And there are distinctive varieties of service and ministration, but it is the same Lord [Who is served].*

⁶ *And there are distinctive varieties of operation [of working to accomplish things], but it is the same God Who inspires and energizes them all in all.*

⁷ *But to each one is given the manifestation of the [Holy] Spirit [the evidence, the spiritual illumination of the Spirit] for good and profit.*

⁸ *To one is given in and through the [Holy] Spirit [the power to speak] a message of wisdom, and to another [the power to express] a word of knowledge and understanding according to the same [Holy] Spirit;*

⁹ *To another [wonder-working] faith by the same [Holy] Spirit, to another the extraordinary powers of healing by the one Spirit;*

¹⁰ *To another the working of miracles, to another prophetic insight (the gift of interpreting the divine will and purpose); to another the ability to discern and distinguish between [the utterances of true] spirits [and false ones], to another various kinds of [unknown] tongues, to another the ability to interpret [such] tongues.*

¹¹ *All these [gifts, achievements, abilities] are inspired and brought to pass by one and the same [Holy] Spirit, Who apportions to each person individually [exactly] as He chooses.*

1 Corinthians 12:1-11 (AMP)

Looking at *verses 8-10* very closely, there are nine manifestations of the Spirit highlighted. We have, *the word of wisdom; the word of knowledge; faith; the gifts of healing; the working of miracles; prophecy; discerning of spirits; divers kinds of tongues; the interpretation of tongues.* All these manifestations, commonly called the gifts of the Spirit are gifts that God has given the Church to demonstrate that indeed the Spirit is alive within His people and that the Church is a living Organisation. A body without the spirit and soul is a dead body. In like manner, a Church without visible signs of the indwelling Spirit of God is a dead Church.

What is an outpouring of the Spirit?

While Jesus was on earth, He gave a commandment to his disciples. He told them in *Luke 24:49, "And, behold, I send the promise of my Father upon you: but tarry ye in the city of Jerusalem, until ye be endued with power from on high."* There are times in the life of a person or people when the vital presence of God within becomes visible for all to see. For the disciples, this experience came on the day of Pentecost (*Acts 2:1*). Even though the Holy Spirit lives within the believer every single moment, the physical manifestation of this indwelling is not apparent every single moment. The manifestations of the Spirit are divided to every man severally as He (the Spirit) wills (*1 Corinthians 12:11*). Apostle Peter in his second epistle also highlights times when there are "movings" of the Spirit.

> [19] *We have also a more sure word of prophecy; whereunto ye do well that ye take heed, as unto a light that shineth in a dark place, until the day dawn, and the day star arise in your hearts:*
> [20] *Knowing this first, that no prophecy of the scripture is of any private interpretation.*
> [21] *For the prophecy came not in old time by the will of man: but holy men of God spake as they were moved by the Holy Ghost.*
>
> *2 Peter 1:19-21*

These "movings" of the Spirit, sometimes are sustained over days, months and even years and then appear to subside. These moments of sustained manifestations are the periods I refer to as periods of an *Outpouring of the Spirit*. These are moments when manifestations of the Spirit are like a light that shines in a dark place. A greater manifestation than what currently obtains becomes the norm. This does not necessarily mean that there were no manifestations of the Spirit. No, not at all. It just means that a greater dimension of the Spirit is present that makes the old seem like darkness. Even though this New Testament dispensation of grace overrides the law of Moses, God was still the giver of the Law. God reveals Himself line upon line and precept upon precept.

Before we leave this concept of "Outpouring of the Spirit" and look at some patterns in the Scriptures, there is a vital point I need to make here. In the description of the manifestations of the Spirit in *1 Corinthians 12*, notice how Paul uses the terms, "to one", "to another" and "by the same Spirit." Though these terms appear to be used to describe the different manifestations, they also say a lot more.

To one and to another
During an outpouring of the Spirit, all the gifts are not necessarily poured on a single individual. The manifestations are spread across "to one" and "to another." I strongly believe that any outpouring that focuses attention on one individual without the possibility of spreading to others is not of God. The terms also highlight the fact that during an outpouring, believers may act differently based on the different stirring of the Spirit within.

The fact that one person or group of people do not manifest the Spirit like we do does not mean they are not operating under the influence of the Holy Spirit. People have introduced denominationalism on the basis of these differences of administrations, diversities of operations and diversities of gifts. We should always remember that all these manifestations, operations and administrations are by the same Spirit. Every outpouring of the Spirit should bring unity to the Body of Christ

The Gift of Prophecy

In the context of an Outpouring of the Spirit, one of the gifts that takes centre stage is the gift of prophecy. The first manifestation of the Spirit after an outpouring is the gift of prophecy. This gift is also one of the gifts that is often misunderstood by present-day Christians. If you have been praying for an outpouring, the minute you see the gift of prophecy in manifestation, gather yourself together because you are about to be hit by a storm of the Spirit. Someone may ask why I say prophecy takes centre stage. My answer is very simple.

When the promise of an outpouring was given to the prophet Joel, God was very specific about what the immediate results were going be. Let us look at what the prophet said in Joel 2:28-32.

> *28 And it shall come to pass afterward, that I will pour out my spirit upon all flesh; and your sons and your daughters shall prophesy, your old men shall dream dreams, your young men shall see visions:*
> *29 And also upon the servants and upon the handmaids in those days will I pour out my spirit.*
> *30 And I will shew wonders in the heavens and in the earth, blood, and fire, and pillars of smoke.*
> *31 The sun shall be turned into darkness, and the moon into blood, before the great and terrible day of the Lord come.*

³² And it shall come to pass, that whosoever shall call on the name of the Lord shall be delivered: for in mount Zion and in Jerusalem shall be deliverance, as the Lord hath said, and in the remnant whom the Lord shall call.

Joel 2:28-32

Looking at *verse 28* very closely, we see, clearly, what God said will happen after He had poured his Spirit upon all flesh.

1. *Your sons shall prophesy*

2. *Your daughters shall prophesy*

3. *Old men shall dream dreams*

4. *Young men shall see visions*

5. *Wonders in the Heaven and the Earth, Blood, fire and pillars of smoke, The sun shall be turned in darkness, The moon shall be turned into blood*

6. *Whosoever shall call on the name of the Lord shall be saved*

I believe one reason prophecy is important is that Prophecy in the New Testament really deals with *Edifying, Exhorting* and *Comforting* the people of God. We will not go into the difference between Prophecy in the Old Testament and what we have in the New Testament here but prophecy builds up the people of God. It is inspired utterances given at specific times to people or groups. It is speaking by inspiration, the divine will and mind of God to set men on the path of life. Let us look at some examples in the Scriptures

⁶⁷ And his father Zacharias was filled with the Holy Ghost, and prophesied, saying,

Zacharias was filled with the Holy Ghost, and prophesied. What he said next shows us what prophecy is like. Remember, *Edification, Exhortation* and *Comfort.* The JB Phillips translation makes a clear distinction between prophecy and the office of the Prophet. Look at *verse 67.*

> *67, Then Zacharias, his father, filled with the Holy Spirit and speaking like a prophet, (JB Phillips)*

Zacharias was speaking like a prophet but was not necessarily a prophet.

> *68 Blessed be the Lord God of Israel; for he hath visited and redeemed his people,*
> *69 And hath raised up an horn of salvation for us in the house of his servant David;*
> *70 As he spake by the mouth of his holy prophets, which have been since the world began:*
> *71 That we should be saved from our enemies, and from the hand of all that hate us;*
> *72 To perform the mercy promised to our fathers, and to remember his holy covenant;*
> *73 The oath which he sware to our father Abraham,*
> *74 That he would grant unto us, that we being delivered out of the hand of our enemies might serve him without fear,*
> *75 In holiness and righteousness before him, all the days of our life.*

Up until this point, Zacharias had not really said anything that could not have been picked up from the pages of *the Laws and the Prophets* as they were called them in those days. These are comforting and uplifting words that reminded the people about the God they served. It highlighted the special place they had with God. The message, thus far is really general. It was not until the next verse before Zacharias switches to talking about the child specifically.

76 And thou, child, shalt be called the prophet of the Highest: for thou shalt go before the face of the Lord to prepare his ways;
77 To give knowledge of salvation unto his people by the remission of their sins,
78 Through the tender mercy of our God; whereby the dayspring from on high hath visited us,
79 To give light to them that sit in darkness and in the shadow of death, to guide our feet into the way of peace.

Luke 1:67-79

I hope you noticed the slight change in the tone of the message. Zacharias, who is speaking like a prophet, now starts to unveil the mind of God concerning the future of the child. Some people would say these verses are moving slightly away from the *gift of prophecy* into another gift of the Spirit called the Word of Wisdom. This may very well be the case. Remember, Zacharias is speaking *"like a prophet."* So this second and higher level gift could have been in manifestation under the prophetic unction. Zacharias was not specifically called a prophet and given we are told he was *"speaking like a prophet,"* he probably was not one. It is not uncommon for people who get around certain types of anointing to get influenced by the atmosphere. Look at what happened to Saul in the Old Testament.

19 And it was told Saul, saying, Behold, David is at Naioth in Ramah.
20 And Saul sent messengers to take David: and when they saw the company of the prophets prophesying, and Samuel standing as appointed over them, the Spirit of God was upon the messengers of Saul, and they also prophesied.
21 And when it was told Saul, he sent other messengers, and they prophesied likewise. And Saul sent messengers again the third time, and they prophesied also.
22 Then went he also to Ramah, and came to a great well that is in Sechu: and he asked and said, Where are Samuel and David? And

one said, Behold, they be at Naioth in Ramah.

²³ And he went thither to Naioth in Ramah: and the Spirit of God was upon him also, and he went on, and prophesied, until he came to Naioth in Ramah.

²⁴ And he stripped off his clothes also, and prophesied before Samuel in like manner, and lay down naked all that day and all that night. Wherefore they say, Is Saul also among the prophets?

1 Samuel 19:19-24

Remember, the point we are making here. Very often in Scriptures when people get filled with the Spirit, the first gift to manifest is the *gift of prophecy*. Look at another example.

²⁴ And Moses went out, and told the people the words of the Lord, and gathered the seventy men of the elders of the people, and set them round about the tabernacle.

25 And the Lord came down in a cloud, and spake unto him, and took of the spirit that was upon him, and gave it unto the seventy elders: and it came to pass, that, when the spirit rested upon them, they prophesied, and did not cease.

²⁶ But there remained two of the men in the camp, the name of the one was Eldad, and the name of the other Medad: and the spirit rested upon them; and they were of them that were written, but went not out unto the tabernacle: and they prophesied in the camp.

²⁷ And there ran a young man, and told Moses, and said, Eldad and Medad do prophesy in the camp.

Numbers 11:24-27

If we look at *verses 28-29*, it almost appears that Joshua was afraid of what was going on.

²⁸ And Joshua the son of Nun, the servant of Moses, one of his young men, answered and said, My lord Moses, forbid them.

²⁹ And Moses said unto him, Enviest thou for my sake? would God that all the Lord's people were prophets, and that the Lord would put his spirit upon them!

Numbers 11:28-29

Moses recognised the fact the people will generally prophesy when the Spirit of God comes upon them.

The strength of the New Testament is that this experience is not only for those appointed into offices but for everyone. Joel said, "..*Your sons and your daughters shall prophesy...*"

There is yet another story in the Old Testament that shows the link between the Holy Spirit coming upon people and the *gift of prophecy.*

> [1] *Then Samuel took a vial of oil, and poured it upon his head, and kissed him, and said, Is it not because the Lord hath anointed thee to be captain over his inheritance?*
> [2] *When thou art departed from me to day, then thou shalt find two men by Rachel's sepulchre in the border of Benjamin at Zelzah; and they will say unto thee, The asses which thou wentest to seek are found: and, lo, thy father hath left the care of the asses, and sorroweth for you, saying, What shall I do for my son?*
> [3] *Then shalt thou go on forward from thence, and thou shalt come to the plain of Tabor, and there shall meet thee three men going up to God to Bethel, one carrying three kids, and another carrying three loaves of bread, and another carrying a bottle of wine:*
> [4] *And they will salute thee, and give thee two loaves of bread; which thou shalt receive of their hands.*
> [5] *After that thou shalt come to the hill of God, where is the garrison of the Philistines: and it shall come to pass, when thou art come thither to the city, that thou shalt meet a company of prophets coming down from the high place with a psaltery, and a tabret, and a pipe, and a harp, before them; and they shall prophesy:*
> [6] *And the Spirit of the Lord will come upon thee, and thou shalt prophesy with them, and shalt be turned into another man.*
> [7] *And let it be, when these signs are come unto thee, that thou do as occasion serve thee; for God is with thee.*
> [8] *And thou shalt go down before me to Gilgal; and, behold, I will come down unto thee, to offer burnt offerings, and to sacrifice sacrifices of peace offerings: seven days shalt thou tarry, till I come*

to thee, and shew thee what thou shalt do.

⁹ *And it was so, that when he had turned his back to go from Samuel, God gave him another heart: and all those signs came to pass that day.*

¹⁰ *And when they came thither to the hill, behold, a company of prophets met him; and the Spirit of God came upon him, and he prophesied among them.*

¹¹ *And it came to pass, when all that knew him beforetime saw that, behold, he prophesied among the prophets, then the people said one to another, What is this that is come unto the son of Kish? Is Saul also among the prophets?*

¹² *And one of the same place answered and said, But who is their father? Therefore it became a proverb, Is Saul also among the prophets?*

¹³ *And when he had made an end of prophesying, he came to the high place.*

1 Samuel 10:1-13

This phenomenon was not only an Old Testament occurrence. Excluding Pentecost, there are also examples in the New Testament.

¹ *And it came to pass, that, while Apollos was at Corinth, Paul having passed through the upper coasts came to Ephesus: and finding certain disciples,*

² *He said unto them, Have ye received the Holy Ghost since ye believed? And they said unto him, We have not so much as heard whether there be any Holy Ghost.*

³ *And he said unto them, Unto what then were ye baptized? And they said, Unto John's baptism.*

⁴ *Then said Paul, John verily baptized with the baptism of repentance, saying unto the people, that they should believe on him which should come after him, that is, on Christ Jesus.*

⁵ *When they heard this, they were baptized in the name of the Lord Jesus.*

6 And when Paul had laid his hands upon them, the Holy Ghost came on them; and they spake with tongues, and prophesied.

Acts 19:1-6

⁶ And as Paul laid his hands upon them, the Holy Spirit came on them; and they spoke in [foreign, unknown] tongues (languages) and prophesied.

Acts 19:6 (AMP)

Even in the New Testament, the *gift of prophecy* very often follows the infilling of the Spirit.

www.ingramcontent.com/pod-product-compliance
Lightning Source LLC
Chambersburg PA
CBHW032014040426

42448CB00006B/638